WE WERE THE FUTURE

WE WERE
THE FUTURE

A MEMOIR OF THE KIBBUTZ

YAEL NEEMAN

TRANSLATED FROM THE HEBREW BY SONDRA SILVERSTON

POEMS AND SONGS TRANSLATED BY JESSICA COHEN

OVERLOOK DUCKWORTH
NEW YORK • LONDON

First published in hardcover in the United States and the United Kingdom in 2016 by
Overlook Duckworth, Peter Mayer Publishers, Inc.

NEW YORK
141 Wooster Street
New York, NY 10012
www.overlookpress.com
For bulk and special sales please contact sales@overlookny.com,
or write us at the above address.

LONDON
30 Calvin Street, London E1 6NW
E: info@duckworth-publishers.co.uk
www.ducknet.co.uk
For bulk and special sales please contact sales@duckworth-publishers.co.uk,
or write to us at the above address.

Cataloging-in-Publication Data is available from the Library of Congress
A catalogue record for this book is available from the British Library

Typeset by Edwin Vazquez

Manufactured in the United States of America

ISBN 978-1-4683-1356-7 (US)
ISBN 978-0-7156-5188-9 (UK)

2 4 6 8 10 9 7 5 3 1

WE WERE THE FUTURE

1

We were always telling ourselves our story.

Compulsively. Out loud. All the time. Sometimes we got tired even before we began, but we still told it for hours. We listened to each other intently. Because every time we told the story we learned new details. Even years later, when we were no longer there.

For example, we hadn't known that some of the kids from the Pine group, who were five years older than we were, worked with the cowboys. And that they lived in an enclave of Hungarian rural life within our kibbutz. We hadn't known that instead of saying good morning and goodnight, they said *lofes* (a horse's prick). We hadn't known that Itai, one of the Pine group, freely rode a horse around our hills when he was only six years old.

The stories were told only orally, contrary to all written rules. They rose from the lawn sprinklers that surrounded the dining room, from the scorched remains of our Crusader fortress, from the cracks of the beautiful, narrow stone sidewalks. We told our stories with shining eyes. We said, "It's unbelievable that they used to slaughter the cows on the ramp, right in front of us, that they used to decapitate the chickens like it was nothing at all," but we spoke as if those were the best years of our lives.

And they really were the best years of our lives, dipped in gold, precisely because we lived in below-zero temperatures in the blazing heat of an eternal sun. We greeted each new day with eagerness and curiosity. We were wide awake in the morning and wide awake at night. We skipped and ran from place to place, our hands sticky with pine tree resin and fig milk. We were so close to each other, all day and all night. Yet we knew nothing about ourselves.

We always told our story, even then, in the children's house on nights when the full moon glowed orange in the sky. Even then, day and night, so we could sleep, so we wouldn't sleep, we'd sit in the corridor at the doors to our rooms or on our beds and exaggerate to death the stories of our city vacations with our biological families. (We traveled with our mothers, fathers, sisters and brothers. For a week, we were a city family, dressed in the fancy travel clothes that were handed down from one child to another for traveling to the city.) When we came back, each one separately, from the kibbutz apartment on Sheinkin Street in Tel Aviv, we told each other about the same Medrano Circus we all went to. Except that the night we were at the circus with our biological family was different from the other nights—that night, the lions escaped from their cage, the tightrope walker fell off the rope—that's what we said. We told each other stories that were totally unrelated to reality.

Sometimes, after we'd left the kibbutz, we tried to tell our story to city people. We weren't able to get it across, neither the plot nor the tone. Our voices grated like the off-key recorder playing of our childhood, too high or too low. We gave up in the middle. The words fell, hollow, between us and the city people the way the stitches fell from our mothers' knitting needles as they sat silently beside their talking husbands during the Saturday night kibbutz meetings.

We spoke in the plural. That's how we were born, that's how we grew up, forever. Our horizons were strange, bent.

From the moment we were released from the hospital, they never tried to separate us. On the contrary, they joined us, glued us, welded us together.

The Narcissus children in the nursery; Yael is pictured first from the left.

But that being welded together wasn't the main thing, even if people who talk about their childhood on the kibbutz sometimes think it is. It was merely a byproduct of the experiment with socialism. (The decision regarding communal sleeping arrangements was taken in 1918 and applied to all the kibbutzim, except for some of the older ones—Degania Aleph, Degania Bet and Ein Harod—who opposed it. They were exempt. Degania was there first, even before the system and the regulations.)

Their intention wasn't to weld, but just the opposite, to separate; to separate the children from the oppressive weight of their parents, who would pamper them and impose their wills on them with mother's milk and father's ambitions. To separate and protect the children from the bourgeois nature of the family. "We will change henceforth the old tradition," as the Internationale proclaimed, and a different, more just and egalitarian world would rise, like a phoenix, from its ashes. That was their declared intention and hope—that the new child would grow into a new kind of person. The longing of some of the kibbutz children for the family they never had was the longing for an idea we had no inkling of, like, for instance, the longing of the Jews in the Diaspora for Jerusalem.

I was in the second grade when I saw an adult wearing pajamas for the first time. It was my father, who had fallen asleep during the afternoon shift. We went to our parents' rooms every day from 5:30 to 7:20 in the evening, a total of one hour and fifty minutes (until the seventh grade, when they sent us away to an educational institution in Evron). At 5:30 that day I went into their room without knocking (we didn't knock on any doors, and ours were always open twenty-four hours a day—after all, there was nothing to hide; the houses belonged to all of us, they weren't a bourgeois possession to be guarded and fortified), and he was asleep in bed wearing pajamas. I ran outside, my pulse racing, and yelled that my father was dead. He's dead. Someone saw me on the sidewalk and, concerned, went inside to check. Zvi N. is not dead, Zvi is sleeping. That's how grown-ups look when they're sleeping: they lie quietly on their beds, their faces to the wall, their backs to us, wearing enormous pajamas and covered with a piqué blanket.

Our story appeared to be only a plot, a plot that was the system, which suited neither children nor adults. Our parents lived alongside it and we lived under it. No one actually lived inside it because it was not meant to house people, only their ambitions and dreams. But we and our parents tried with all our hearts to live inside it; that was the experiment. Our system couldn't be satisfied. We were in awe of it, and we knew that we would never totally succeed. We worshipped it day and night, the older generation (our parents) in the hundreds of vacation days they accumulated, the fruit of their endless labors. And we in the fields, in the dining room, in the children's house. Everywhere.

We knew nothing about the grown-ups' lives, neither about their waking hours nor about their sleep. They inhabited a different planet from ours.

We moved in front of each other like two rows of dancers who grew closer and farther apart from each other in the measured steps of the Friday night dances held in the dining room. We with our flowery group names: Narcissus, Anemone, Squill. They with their group names, which represented the fulfillment of their ideals: The First of May, Stalin, Meadow, Workers. We with our first names, fresh with dew and raindrops: Yael, Michal, Tamar, Ronen. They with their names recently Hebraicized from the Hungarian: from Freddie to Zvi, Aggie to Naomi, Latsi to Itzhak.

We existed in parallel universes—we lived with the Children's Society, our parents with the grown-ups.

We moved in large masses, like a flock of birds, like a herd of zebras, always in two large groups. All the children went together to their daily 5:30 visits, walking each other to their biological parents' houses, and one hour and fifty minutes later, at 7:20, we walked back along the same paths with our parents, who returned us to the children's houses.

We ate our supper in the children's house. They ate theirs in the dining room.

Even before then, right after we were born, we were sent straight from the hospital to the babies' house, to the *metapelet*[1] who was waiting there for the mothers. They used to come to nurse together, sitting one next to the other, always at the same time. The synchronization was meant to guarantee that no child got more. Not less and not more. The parents arrived in flocks at bedtime too, for the quarter of an hour they were allowed. Not all of them came, because bedtime was the same in all the children's houses, and apart from that, many of them were busy building the kibbutz, sitting on committees. We moved before them with wheat sheaves in our hands on Rosh Hashanah, we acted out the *Hadgadya* song on Passover, threading our way among the long tables to the stage in our festive clothes. We came together in the well-orchestrated choreography, unknowingly following the instructions in the loose-leaf binders of detailed plans

---

[1] "The person who takes care of," the *metapelet* is the caregiver for children on the kibbutz, whose role was to be responsible for the children's everyday routine.

for celebrating the holidays that were sent to all Hashomer Hatzair[2] kibbutzim and then adapted by the Holiday Committee to suit its particular kibbutz. We made fleeting incursions into their nightlives on holidays and left "with timbres and with dances [...] the horse and his rider hath He thrown into the sea," in the unique steps created for us by Nira. (All kibbutz children were doing the same thing at exactly the same time, celebrating the Hashomer Hatzair Pessach Haggadah.) We danced before them on the lawn, at end-of-year school shows, and on the kibbutz holiday we sang, "We're building a kibbutz of beauty, the likes of which you never did see, the likes of which you never did see."

The Narcissus children at the beach; Yael is pictured second from the left.

---

2 A youth movement based on socialist ideology founded in 1913 in Eastern Europe; Hashomer Hatzair members believed that the liberation of Jewish youth could only be accomplished by immigration to Palestine and living in kibbutzim.

7

They, the adults, sang too. They sang in harmony in a choir, danced the Chassidic dances that were danced at weddings on all Hashomer Hatzair kibbutzim, without a rabbi. (The couples went to the Rabbinate in Nahariya, got formally married and came back for the parties so that the rabbi wouldn't set foot on the kibbutz, so that their religion wouldn't touch our religion.)

Four couples get married. The grown-ups dance and we stand there with wreaths on our heads, large branches forming a gate for the pairs of chosen children, and we sing Kadya Molodovski, the city woman whose words accompanied our lives, like a melody: "Open the gate, open it wide, like a golden chain, we'll go inside: father and mother, sister and brother, groom and bride, in a chariot we all will ride."

We sang, we danced, we played the recorder, the mandolin and the cymbals, and when the artistic program was over, we all went back to our places. The lawn emptied out, the door to the dining room closed behind us, and we returned to our little world in the Narcissus house with its little bathrooms, its little beds, its little tables, surrounded by the Children's Society—Anemone under us and Terebinth above us. We were happy.

At night we dreamt about the heroes of Eric Kästner's stories that our *metapelet* read to us from nine until nine twenty every evening, sitting in the corridor, only her voice audible, we in our beds. Noriko-san, the little girl from Japan, was exactly our age.

Sometimes our dreams were chaotic. Scary stories we were told remained hanging above us like a black cloud. The *metapelet* said goodnight and left, closing the door behind her, and we were awake. Frightened. As if the Red Everlasting flower pin that we loved with every ounce of our being had penetrated the white shirts we wore on holidays, piercing our skin. And we waited for the light to come so we could run outside. We were always allowed to escape from classes, as in enlightened countries where prisoners who escape are not tried because it is the nature of man to try to escape from prison, to be free. In the middle of our lessons, we sailed on boards in our reservoir pond. Sometimes we got up at night, sat at the doors to our rooms and spoke or played. We couldn't fall asleep. Once, we lit a bonfire in our dining room and went back to our beds. There were no grown-ups in our world at night.

2

Actually, the story of our creation, the creation of the new world, never happened. Maybe that was why we told it to ourselves over and over again. We didn't have a written language or one that we could use to translate our lives for the city people.

We thought that multitudes would join us. Groups from Hashomer Hatzair, volunteers from overseas, workers of the world. We didn't know that, in 1960, we were born to a star whose light had long since died and it was now on its way to the sea. We didn't know that the kibbutz movement had been at the height of its prestige during the Wall-and-Tower period in the 1930s, and that before the establishment of the state in 1947, the kibbutz population was the highest it would ever be—7% of the entire Jewish population. In

The Narcissus group on an excursion;
Yael pictured fifth from right, the smallest child wearing the hat.

'48, we were already decreasing, and in the '70s, we were only 3.3%
of the entire population.

We didn't know that our star illuminated only itself. We thought
that we were growing and building.

We were born in 1960 on Kibbutz Yehiam, the most beautiful
kibbutz in the world—green with pines, purple with Judas trees, yellow with broom plants—founded in 1946 on a hill below a Crusader
fortress. We were born to the Narcissus Group. We were sixteen children in Narcissus, eight boys and eight girls. We were a gentle group,
most of us born to older parents, the Hungarian founders of the kibbutz who built it together with an Israeli group of Hashomer Hatzair.

We said the names of the children in our group quickly, all strung
together, in order of age. There was also the alphabetical order of
surnames, the bourgeois order that could only be used by strangers

who didn't know anything, or by doctors, when, for instance, we were waiting our turn to see the dentist who came from Nahariya or the Krayot near Haifa. In an indifferent tone, he used to dictate to Miriam Ron, who was in charge of the clinic, the bad news that was repeated every year: seven cavities, or nine, or twelve. We had so many cavities and so few sweets. And we all wore braces made for us by the orthodontist. We also waited on line for him until Miriam called us in the alphabetical order of our surnames, and he too came from Nahariya or the Krayot.

We hadn't exactly chosen the name Narcissus, even though we did ultimately vote for it, unanimously, in the first grade. The group's name went with us everywhere—it hung on the bulletin board and was written on the name tag sewed onto our clothes in the *communa*, the clothing supply room. Every group had its own color and its own Roman numeral. We were brown and our number was X.

When we chose the name, we still weren't familiar with the rules. We didn't understand that we had to have the names of flowers or something else in nature. When we were born, there were already about 120 children on the kibbutz, divided into groups by age. And although the groups before us were called Rock, Grove, Cyclamen, Pomegranate, Pine, Oak and Terebinth, we still didn't understand. We never noticed.

We suggested a variety of names, most of them ending with "Gang." "The Explosion Gang," "The Forest Gang," and all the other adventurous sounding names. The *metapelet* directed us, at first gently, then more firmly to the world of flowers until we fell into line and chose Narcissus. I don't remember the name of the other flower we were considering; I think we already realized that it didn't matter if we were Narcissus, Anemone or Chrysanthemum—the names given to the groups that came after us. We understood that it was like choosing white or carrot-orange sandals that had the same shape.

Other kibbutzim like ours throughout the country, from the Galilee to the Negev, chose the same names. And we all dreamed about Noriko-san, the little girl from Japan.

Fishel from Nahariya was the kibbutz barber.

Every once in a while, at intervals that we could not understand, he would come to us, the Narcissus Group. Amongst ourselves, we called him Dr. Fishel, maybe because of Dr. Zuriel, the kibbutz doctor, who also came from Nahariya, and Dr. Pollack, his replacement who also came from Nahariya, and Dr. Lieber, the dentist. We thought that maybe everyone in Nahariya was a doctor. But Fishel

Fishel, the kibbutz barber, at work.

wasn't a doctor; nor was he one of the Naharyia Yekkim, the Jews of German descent who lived in that city. He was Fishel the Barber, and he lived in the transit camp next to the Nahariya hospital.

We hated having our hair cut, but we suffered mainly from Fishel's lies. It never occurred to us that you could lie without blinking an eye and even repeat the same lies over and over again. We sat in regular chairs for our haircuts. There were no adults around and we really didn't understand the order in which we were called. Whenever it was another child's turn, the sheet was flapped around his shoulders like a bib, quickly, and there wasn't a lot of time to be afraid. It was clear that after he left us, Fishel moved on with his equipment to cut other children's hair. Only much later did we learn, almost by chance, that all the professionals—the barbers, doctors, dentists—worked not only with the children, but with all the kibbutz members. They came, worked for a flat rate, and left.

As he worked, Fishel asked each child what he wanted: Balloons? Candy? Then he memorized each answer (or so we thought) and promised to bring balloons or candy on his next visit. That's how it was every time. And he never brought anything. But we believed him each time and cried with disappointment when no gifts arrived the next time either. Fishel, after all, came from Nahariya, a city that was all candy and chocolate-coated bananas in the stores and rolls and butter in Hans and Gila's café. Enchanting coaches drawn by horses rolled along Haga'aton Boulevard, whisking passengers from one place to another. All the best things in the world were there, and he probably never gave us a thought as he walked past all the display windows.

But Fishel must have hated us much more than we hated him, and he certainly didn't have the money to buy us presents. We didn't even know whether he had children of his own. We didn't know a thing about the homes of our dentists in Haifa and the Krayot; we thought that all the city people were rich. We didn't know that they worked at a flat rate and lived in transit camps.

We drowned in a sea of our own sweat. The sounds of the recorders, mandolins and cymbals deafened us. We were burned by the banner of letters that were doused in kerosene and set aflame: "For Zionism, Socialism and the Brotherhood Amongst Nations," like the slogan of the newspaper *Al Hamishmar* that was put in our parents' mailboxes everyday. But we never connected that to our neighbors in Yanuh, the Druze village visible at the edge of the horizon on the eastern side of the fortress. We used to go hiking there with our teacher, crossing our *wadi*, the Yehiam stream, hearing about the arbutus and Judas trees, and, in a demonstration of the brotherhood amongst nations, walked up to Yanuh's enormous school for a visit. There, they always gave us brightly-colored candy and invited us to see their classes. We reciprocated by inviting them to visit us. When they came, we gave them wafers. We played soccer. We beat them by so much, 13:1 or 12:0, that we were dizzy with victory for days.

We didn't know that thousands of people lived in Yanuh, that the town had no infrastructure, that they had to study Bialik, the Hebrew poet. They told us, but we didn't study Bialik, so we didn't understand what that meant. We knew nothing. Neither Hebrew nor Arabic. Yanuh was two kilometers away, but light-years separated us.

And we knew nothing about our neighbors in the development town of Ma'alot, except that, starting in the seventh grade, we had to help them with their homework once a week for two hours. We knew nothing about Lebanon on the other side of the border.

We knew nothing about Kabri either, the kibbutz we had to pass on the way to see the doctors in the Kupat Holim clinic in Nahariya. Because Kabri wasn't in Hashomer Hatzair.

We walked around like *fakirs,*[3] both children and adults, on the surface of a moon nobody wanted to discover. We believed that we would pluck stars and the stars, like fireworks, would light up the skies over all the countries in the world. And workers would march by their light as if they were torches, and equality and justice would descend upon the world. Our legs hurt so much from the effort that we could focus only on the march itself. We forgot who we were bringing equality to, who we were forging peace with and who deserved justice. We drank our sweat and helped no one.

Volunteers used to come to us from all over the world. They came on their school vacations, filled with enthusiasm about what was called "lending a hand," helping us with our work. We played volleyball with them, spoke our broken English, played guitars, tried lying on a waterbed. Look, the world is coming to us, so blond, fair and polite. They worked, took an interest in our lives and then went back overseas. We went on with our lives.

---

3 Derived from the Arabic word for "poverty," a religious ascetic who performs stunts such as walking across broken glass or nails.

3

The old-timers and adults that we, the children, considered important were, in certain cases, totally different from the ones immortal-
ized in the kibbutz's official history, in *The Jubilee Book* or various
other commemorative projects. We already knew when we were
children that on our kibbutz, Yehiam, and on all the kibbutzim from
the Sea of Galilee to the Negev, there was always a rotation in the
higher, desirable positions, such as secretary, work coordinator, and
the like.

We didn't notice, neither then nor later on, that there was no
rotation in other occupations. No one ever asked to switch jobs with
the women who did the laundry; no one ever coveted the Sisyphean
work of the potato peelers, who spent decades sitting on low stools

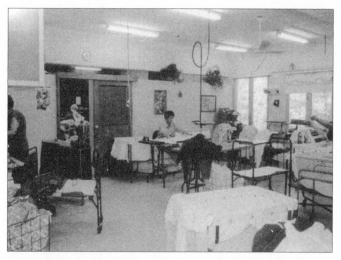

Women working in the *communa*, the clothing storeroom.

Women working in the kitchen.

beside huge pots in the kitchen. There was never any rotation for the woman who cleaned the public showers and toilets for years. On the kibbutzim, those jobs were designated the "service branch" (to differentiate them from the profitable and productive jobs in the fields or factories), like an HQ battalion whose soldiers remain in camp to outfit tanks and prepare food for the hungry officers and troops returning from maneuvers or the battlefield.

Rotation, one of the marvels of our system, protected the prominent members who moved from one major function to another, and turned its back on the members of the lower castes, keeping them trapped in place.

Most of the service providers were from the Workers group. The name hadn't been chosen deliberately to be such a dazzlingly ironic contrast to the First of May group, whose members were among the founders of the kibbutz and members of the movement even before the war, in Hungary.

The members of the Workers group were Zionist refugees of the war who joined Hashomer Hatzair in Hungary after the war, and immigrated to Israel under the movement's sponsorship. They said later: "To this day, it is not clear what had more of an effect on us: the ideological arguments or the good chocolates and cigarettes." They arrived in Yehiam two years after it had been established, several months after the War of Independence battles that had been fought there. They were full partners in the building and development of the kibbutz.

Even after we, members of the kibbutz, left, and even after the volunteers and many members of all the other groups were gone, members of the Workers group remained. The largest percentage of those who remained in Kibbutz Yehiam at any time was from the Hungarian Workers group.

Our contact with the grown-ups was dictated by the logic of our everyday lives and included only those who played a part in them: teachers, *metaplot,*[4] workers in the *communa* (the clothing storeroom), the shoe repair workshop and the dining hall—people from the service branch.

The heroes of our mythology were almost all members of the Workers group because they were the ones who worked on the kibbutz land, in the *communa*, in the kitchen. They were the ones who sometimes stopped beside us on the sidewalk and gave us an affectionate pat. And they were also the only ones who allowed their children to stay in their biological homes for a while after they ran away from the children's house, and gave them candy. We didn't know then that they were from the Workers group, and neither my brothers nor I knew that our mother was from the First of May group and that our father had come to the country earlier, in 1939, after a family council convened in Vienna and decided that all the young people would leave without delay.

After all, the past is irrelevant on kibbutzim. Everyone—whether born in a village in Hungary or in Budapest, in Vienna or Haifa—is equal in the eyes of the system.

The head of the Hungarian old-timers in the Workers group, the leader of all the old-timers, the person in first place, miles ahead of everyone else, was Pirosh. Though he did not take part in the battles with the Arabs in the War of Independence (members of the Workers

---

4 Plural of *metapelet.*

group arrived in Yehiam after that war), or establish an agricultural branch, and was never appointed kibbutz secretary or work coordinator, we knew that without him, the kibbutz would collapse.

Twice a year, a line of our children, like a huge centipede, would go to the shoemaking workshop and try on the new shoes that Pirosh made for us.

Pirosh means "red" or "redhead" in Hungarian, but when we were born, he was already more bald than redheaded. Pirosh cursed whenever he wanted, gave our thighs a hard, painful slap whenever he wanted, and chose his helpers in the *colbo*, where we got supplies, from among the girls in the seventh grade or higher, based on the size of their breasts. He said it as if he were talking about awarding medals to the girls he described as having "large balconies." No one on the kibbutz ever spoke like that, only Pirosh. He was the shoemaker, he chose the movies we saw and screened them, and he was in charge of the weapons storeroom and the *colbo*. Each of those was almost a full-time job.

The shoemaking workshop was a small shed on the edge of the kibbutz, whose walls, and especially its high, slanted ceiling, were covered with pictures of starlets—that's what Pirosh called them—that he clipped from various magazines. All of them were glamorous women with plunging necklines, huge breasts and broad smiles. Pirosh taught us their names. We didn't know whether that shed was really so different from other kibbutz buildings, or whether it seemed so different to us because of the starlets, the smell of leather and the shoe-stretching machines. The workshop consisted of two rooms, and Pirosh sat in the first room with his constant assistant, Meir S., an excellent professional shoemaker, who people said had also been one in Hungary. Meir S. would stop working only to smile his bashful smile and ask how we were, and he was never irritable. They sat on either side of a huge worktable that was littered with tools and shoe parts.

They worked with their entire bodies, and their mouths were always full of nails, as were all their pockets.

The other room contained the stretching machines, many boxes of shoes, and two small stools on which we would sit in front of Pirosh to try on the new line he made for us twice every year—high shoes in winter and sandals in summer. We came to choose a color: sandals in white or carrot-orange for girls, and brown for boys; shoes in red or brown for all of us. The shape was the same for all the children of the Kibbutz Artzi movement.

No one knew exactly what Pirosh's story was. He was such a presence that questions seemed unnecessary. But we asked anyway. Pirosh was single. Sometimes our centipede, shod in red or brown, would stop near a group of old-timers and ask why Pirosh was single, why he didn't have any children. They didn't answer us. It was as if our question passed, like a paper plane, over the heads of those busy people rushing from place to place, without ever landing. He was single, and that was that. Once, someone told us that it was a case of unrequited love. We considered every aspect of that answer, but couldn't remember who said it and whether he really meant it. Maybe he just wanted to get rid of us. Non-practical matters were never discussed. Nor were Pirosh's hard, painful slaps of our thighs when he measured our new shoes and explained: "I'm measuring you thoroughly." We laughed at his jokes, collected them and repeated them over and over again.

The Narcissus group preparing bread in the backyard.

Pirosh pronounced all the names of Hollywood actors and ac-
tresses with a Hungarian accent, and we thought that not only did
he know their names, but he actually knew them. The pictures that
lined the walls of the shoemaking workshop revealed to us the cleavage of Raquel Welch and company, and in that décolletage, we saw
an escape, a hint that a different kind of life was possible. The idea
of hanging pictures of women with their cleavage exposed was so out
of the ordinary that Hashomer Hatzair did not have a clause in its
rules of conduct prohibiting it. And that's another reason we were
so proud of Pirosh. In our heart of hearts, we knew that he worked
an additional job for us that was much more important than all
the other services he provided: For us, he symbolized the existence
of other worlds—*L'Hiton* (an entertainment magazine), Tel Aviv,
Hollywood and New York. As if he were actually a subversive one-
man international commune, a clever one never seen as dangerous

because it never had to declare itself. That's why no one noticed how much Pirosh's existence and his pictures seeped into our minds.

Pirosh's various occupations allowed him to travel a great deal, though never at the expense of work, as he always pointed out. He merely took advantage of the hundreds of vacation days the old-timers had accumulated, the fruit of their endless labors. He went to Tel Aviv, where he saw dozens of movies. Then he brought them to us from the Movie Department.

Until the end of the sixth grade, we saw the movies with the Children's Society. Apart from his job of choosing and screening the movies, Pirosh was also in charge of censoring them. There were no parents, *metaplot* or teachers at the screenings. Only we and Pirosh were there, like in the shoemaking workshop.

Every other week, he brought a movie from Tel Aviv: *Annie Get Your Gun*, *Lassie Come Home*, *Winnetou*, *Chitty Chitty Bang Bang*. He didn't censor vulgarities, only frightening scenes. When a scene he considered frightening was about to appear on the screen, Pirosh would simply order all the children in the third grade and below to leave. That's why we never saw the Wicked Witch in *The Wizard of Oz*. Suddenly he turned on the lights and sent us out.

When we were in the seventh grade, we joined the adults on movie night, which the entire kibbutz eagerly awaited. Once a week we'd sit in rows in the large dining hall. The screening would be delayed, the way daily lectures and Friday night dinners in the dining hall were delayed, until everyone agreed on whether to open or close the windows. Those arguments were like a silent movie being shown over and over again before the main feature. First the window-closers would get up, and without a word, close them and sit down. Then the window-openers would get up, open them and sit down. The two groups operated in a sequence known only to them.

No one ever intervened, neither the children nor the adults. We all knew that this had also come from there. (Most of the Hungarians, from both The First of May and the Workers groups, came from there. And there—my mother told me once when I was sick—the Danube froze over in winter. And there—another member once told us—the Danube was red with blood because so many Jews had been shot and thrown into it all at once.) Somehow, we all accepted the explanation of the getting-up-and-opening and the getting-up-and-closing offered by one kid in our centipede to another: Anyone who was in the camps or holed up in a cramped hiding place needed to open. Anyone who was in an open area or who was set upon by dogs had to close. We would wait. For those who closed and those who opened.

After the windows issue was resolved, Pirosh would begin the screening, the first reel threaded and ready to go. Carmi, one of his constant apprentices, son of Meir S. from the shoemaking workshop and the only person Pirosh trusted, would help him. Pirosh had begun training him for the job when he was seven.

In the middle or towards the end of the second reel—because the first part of the screening was always longer than the second—Pirosh's voice boomed as he separated the word into individual syllables: IN-TER-MI-SSION. He pronounced the word with the proper diction he'd worked hard to achieve for only that single word and had polished endlessly until it reached perfection. When the five-minute intermission was over, the screening began again with no delays or postponements. Even if the members pleaded, he never waited.

Though Pirosh insisted on good behavior, we could still hear clearly the shouts of the people in the last row who accompanied the movie with a unique soundtrack of comments and jokes.

The Movie Department of the Histadrut Labor Federation, from which all the kibbutzim and *moshavim*[5] took the movies, was located on Sheinkin Street in Tel Aviv, three houses away from our apartment. "Our apartment" on Sheinkin in the center of Tel Aviv wasn't exactly ours, but that's what we, all the kibbutz members and children, called it. All the kibbutzim had apartments in the city, where we vacationed with our biological families, and where the "activists" spent nights—that's what we called the members who worked outside the kibbutz. The nicknames we gave to people who held those positions were always as dynamic as the name of our eternally young movement, Hashomer Hatzair, the Young Guard.

Zili from Ashkelon rented the apartment to Kibbutz Yehiam at a very cheap rate. We thought that Zili was a millionaire. He wasn't a millionaire, but his brother, Diuri, was a member of the Workers group on Kibbutz Yehiam, and he wanted to contribute and help kibbutzim.

We believed that when Pirosh went to Tel Aviv and saw fourteen movies in three days, he thought about which of them would be especially appropriate for us. We didn't know that the decisions were made long before that by the people in the Movie Department of the Histadrut. The movies were passed from one kibbutz to the other. On all of them, just as on our kibbutz, the members gathered

---

5 *Moshavs* are agricultural settlements where the houses and land are privately owned by residents that share common facilities, unlike the kibbutz, which belongs to all its members and has no private property of any kind; *moshav* children live with their parents and attend traditional schools.

once a week in the dining hall—and in summer, on the lawn of the clubhouse—to watch a movie.

Due to copyright agreements, the movies were copied (from 35mm to 16mm) two or three years after their city premieres.

The French people on the kibbutz occasionally held discussions on cinema and politics and ran the Classic Cinema Club, where they discussed Eisenstein or Bertolucci. But they had difficulty finding classic films because those agreements, as well as copyright problems, required the Department to destroy the copies after five years.

On our planet, the present obliterated the past and the future. The classics were destroyed and the contemporary films had not yet been copied for us. We saw all the movies in our own particular order.

It was the Repertoire Committee of the Histadrut Movie Department that chose which movies to copy. The Movie Department had, in fact, a monopoly on 16mm films in Israel.

Not only did the Department lack a large, important part of classic cinema, but erotic movies weren't included in the repertoire either.

The French members protested against that situation at meetings of the Classic Cinema Club. They asked: Why aren't films like *Emanuelle*, *The Last Tango in Paris*, or *What Do You Say to a Naked Lady* allowed to be screened, while every karate movie is in the Department, along with every Western? Are karate movies and all the other bourgeois family movies preferable to erotic films that raise many existential questions, they wondered out loud during a discussion that preceded the screening itself.

After a few years, those movies arrived as well.

Pirosh also ran the projector at the meetings of the Classic Cinema Club. He never got involved in the discussions. He was in favor of screening all the movies in the world.

4

On Saturdays, the men worked in our children's houses. Some of them were our fathers and some were not. The Saturday shift schedule was organized by the work scheduler. (There was a yearly rotation, ensuring that democracy prevailed among the holders of higher positions.)

The work scheduler left a small green note in the mailboxes of the men assigned to the Saturday shift. Written in pencil on the pieces of paper were the date, time and place of their shift. There was no room for argument or negotiation.

As opposed to the special jobs that members were occasionally mobilized to do, everyone knew what the Saturday shifts were: work on every fourth or fifth Saturday doing jobs that had to be done seven days a week (tending to the children in the children's houses, irrigating and harvesting in the fields, operating the dining hall, and so on). An attempt was made to create a more or less permanent rotation so that the workers could gain experience in the job they did only once every four or five weeks.

One of the men who took care of us, the Narcissus group, on Saturdays was Feivel, the kibbutz metalworker. Feivel stood above or beside all the disagreements. Everyone respected him, and he did not belong to the French, Israeli or the Hungarian groups. He was Polish, always wore work clothes, and really did work all the time. It was as if he had stepped out of a socialist-realist painting, or out of the ceramic mural that Yoskeh had built at the entrance to the dining hall—a wall that showed myriad images of workers and tools being brandished in all directions, creating a composition so filled with movement that it wasn't clear what the central image was supposed to be: the worker, perhaps the scythe or the sickle, or maybe even the work itself.

Feivel continued to work even when the workday was over. He cut iron and welded and soldered tables, shelves and other items that people had asked him to make for them privately, and he never said no.

Once, when he was working the Saturday shift with our group, Feivel told us that the Russians were no better than the Americans, and maybe the Americans were better.

"Feivel said that the Americans are a lot better than the Russians," we told each other that evening after he'd gone to the kibbutz meeting.

The men who worked the Saturday shift in the children's houses didn't know how to braid our hair or make French toast for us. We looked forward to Saturdays, and feared them at the same time. We felt as if we were on a Ferris wheel, knowing we should be enjoying it, but waiting for it to finally end, for Sunday to come. We didn't know whether the Saturday workers could even gather our hair into a ponytail that wouldn't loosen immediately, whether we'd arrive at places on time, whether our food would be ready. We stayed awake to tell them when to wake us, even though they knew. We didn't trust them.

Because of the holes that appeared in our daily routine, we hoped to have adventures. But when we did, we were afraid that we'd made them up, afraid that we'd exaggerated the stories so much that they had destroyed even the kernel of truth they were based on. One Saturday, two minutes before we left for the fortress, Shimon began looking for something, didn't find it, and cursed, motherfucker. We talked about that at night, after Shimon had gone—had he cursed or not, were the coins we'd found at the fortress really ancient and would they be displayed at an exhibition, and if they were, would there be any mention of the fact that they were discovered by the Narcissus children? We weren't sure what had really happened. And then there was the drive with Willie, who substituted for one of the regular Saturday workers. He agreed to take all of us, sixteen children, in his small, Israeli-made Sussita van to the Gaaton turn-off. (The members of Gaaton called it the Yehiam turn-off, and we called it the Gaaton turn-off. In any case, there, you could only turn into Kibbutz Gaaton or Kibbutz Yehiam.)

The men who worked the Saturday shift in our children's house also read us bedtime stories from the corridor, before the door to the world of grown-ups was closed at nine thirty, the time when the men would say goodnight and go off to the kibbutz meetings.

There was a kibbutz meeting every Saturday evening. That was one of the only things we knew about the daily routine of the grown-up world, and while they were having their meeting, we, the Narcissus children, held an alternative kibbutz meeting, which we invented. We sat at the doors to our four rooms, wrote minutes, and discussed adding new rules to the games we played at night, for example, "Tushy Sport," in which each one of us had to pull down someone else's pajama bottoms, unless they got away and stood in the doorway. We also discussed whether it was legal to remain standing in the doorway for the rest of the game.

During the kibbutz meetings in the dining hall, the men spoke and the women knitted. What did the members do on the other nights of the week? We didn't know. But the kibbutz meetings determined everything: They not only discussed ideological issues, but they resolved all questions related to everyday life on the kibbutz.

A kibbutz meeting, held every Saturday evening.
The women would knit while the men discussed kibbutz affairs.

Kibbutz meetings were the legislature, the judicial and the executive branch: Every departure from the kibbutz—whether extended or brief, for educational purposes or vacations and trips abroad—required their approval. The same was true for every gift the members received, every piece of furniture they wanted to add to their rooms, or assistance they wanted to give to their children or relatives.

Public and private issues were decided upon at the kibbutz meetings, and committees were elected there. If someone wanted to leave the kibbutz for higher education, the secretariat, the Education Committee and finally, the kibbutz meeting decided whether he would go or wait, and also, what he would study: Did the course of study he wished to pursue correspond to what the kibbutz needed? If it didn't, he had to adjust himself to the needs of the community.

The community was an abstract and concrete entity at one and the same time. It was the sum of things that make up an experiment of enormous proportions to actually live the perfect, day-to-day life of a philosophical or literary text. As if the kibbutz had taken not only the Marxist content, but also its philosophical syntax, and turned it into a code by which everyday life would be lived. (In response to a friend's comment that she couldn't imagine Marx living a life of equality, Marx replied: "The day will come, but we would do well to take leave of this world before it does.")

Usually, the men who worked in the children's houses on Saturdays did not read aloud another chapter in the book that the *metaplot* read from, but made up their own stories. Creativity was highly valued in the kibbutz, and so, for example, we never brought each other readymade birthday gifts. It was always preferable to make a clay vase, even if it came out crooked or ugly, or cut out and embroider the edges of yet another bookmark rather than bring a bourgeois gift, that is, a store-bought one. Based on that same logic, it was better to make an effort and invent a story than to read from the book the *metaplot* read from.

We especially liked the stories made up by Yoash, Netta's father, and Hanoch, Moshik's father. Both Netta and Moshik were in our group. Their families were very close and stood out from the rest of our parents. They had crossed over from one kibbutz movement to another and had come to Yehiam from Kibbutz Palmachim.

We were born in 1960, after the split within the kibbutz movement, after the Prague trials, after the Doctors' trial and the Rosenbergs' trial, all of which took place in '52 and '53 and were added to the list of things that were never spoken about, not with us. Nor did we ever mention the rude awakening in '56 after Stalin's death. We didn't know that our eyes had been opened because we didn't know that we'd been blind, and we certainly didn't know that the light of our beliefs had been eclipsed.

True, we sang the Hapoel anthem: "Flames, rise flame, rise, we pound our sledgehammer all day long, all day long. Flame, we are like you, we are like you, our hearts are red. Red." We didn't know what a sledgehammer was anyway. We sang, in harmony and with conviction of the Budyonny Regiments riding into battle: "Hey hey hey. Cossack cavalry ride into battle." We didn't know that it told of plunderers and rapists on their way to endless fields of slaughter. Nor did we know about Stalin, Lenin and Trotsky, what they had in common and what divided them. We had never heard of the *gulags*,[6] and

---

6 A system of labor camps maintained in the former Soviet Union from 1930 to 1955, known for their harsh and deadly conditions.

we didn't know about the millions whose lives had been destroyed because of faith or belief in one of them and not the other. We knew their names the way we knew the names of the generals in the Israeli Army during that period, after '67 and the Six Day War. We thought they were all heroes who had defeated the Nazis, and now were marching us into a better world: Uzi Narkis, Moshe Dayan, Stalin and Lenin.

We knew that we believed in the human spirit and expansive lawns. Who could say no to the human spirit? Who could rise up against expansive lawns?

Moshik and Netta came to us from Kibbutz Palmachim in '62, when we were two years old. We were told that both families moved to our kibbutz for ideological reasons. "Ideological reasons" sounded quite exotic to us, and Moshik and Netta's houses were also exotic. Their parents seemed much younger than ours. They were Israeli, not Hungarian, like ours. The furniture in their houses was completely different from the couches and armchairs made in the Kibbutz Shomrat and Kibbutz Hazorea factory, and different from the veneer book cabinets nailed to the walls of our parents' houses, the shelves lined with books by the Hungarian poets Petofi and Ady, alongside the Even Shoshan Hebrew-Hebrew dictionary.

They had beanbag chairs, an artillery shell vase that held dried thorns, and a couch with pillows on it. Stained glass adorned the windows in Yoash and Malacula's house, Hanoch and Nurit's bell collection chimed, and mobiles hung from their ceiling. The books stood on shelves that rested on bricks, and were interspersed with light and dark blue glass bric-a-bracs. They always gave us refreshments when we came; they spoke differently, laughed differently.

All of us, Hungarians and Israelis alike, were tourists in our biological parents' houses.

Once every five weeks, Hanoch and Yoash did their Saturday shift with us, the Narcissus group. Hanoch told us about Pineto and Tonino, Italian twins from the city of Pisa, who often lost their way in a labyrinth of adventures. Every Saturday evening, he recounted a new adventure, and each adventure had its own labyrinth, which consisted of endless doors.

When, after much hard work and resourcefulness, the twins found the key to one door, they came up against additional doors and gates, each of which had a separate lock. Between one door and the next, and one gate and the next, they sometimes rested and ate spaghetti or pizza. We also rested during those breaks, feeling the taste of the thin-dough pizza in our mouths, and returned to follow the determined twins breathlessly, until each of their complicated adventures came to a successful conclusion and a sweet, happy end, with Pineto and Tonino driving off on their Vespa to have some ice cream.

The absolute opposite happened in Yoash's stories. Yoash didn't believe in happy endings, or in happy beginnings or middles. He was an unpredictable storyteller. He had a deep voice and could emulate many different kinds of speech. His piercing blue eyes added a dramatic dimension to his stories. He was also the kibbutz's best reader. It was his voice that boomed through the loudspeaker on the dining hall stage every Holocaust Day, reading the text about the six million, echoing through the kibbutz as if it were coming from the sky or straight from hell.

Yoash was the kibbutz gardener. In terms of his education and skill, he was much closer to being a landscape or urban architect. He did his gardening job as if his life depended on it, as if he considered "decorative garden," the bureaucratic phrase of kibbutz architecture, the entrance gate to a much wider world. As if he understood, like a Bahaist disguised as a kibbutznik, that underlying the carobs, the lawns and the cyclamens there was an entire religion.

We were afraid of the plot twists that awaited us around the bend in Yoash's stories, especially in the true stories he told us.

Yoash told us every detail of the stories of the Dead Sea Scrolls found in the Judean Desert. He loved to teach us. He didn't decorate his stories with drawings.

On other Saturdays, before he said goodnight and went to the kibbutz meeting, Yoash told us about mountain farming. Yehiam is a mountain farm because it's built on a hill that is more than 400 meters high. That has many implications, some of them economic. For instance, when the fields are far away and you have to drive to them. There are also problems in supplying water to a mountain kibbutz. To illustrate his story, he read us an item that appeared in the newsletter.

Under the title "Stepsons," Yaron, a field worker, wrote:

One of the problems of our kibbutz is that the fields are very far away from the houses. This geographic distance creates a physical and emotional separation, and sometimes we (the field workers) feel like "stepsons" of the kibbutz. I don't want to complain, but I do want to suggest one thing that will improve the situation: making all the kibbutz workers (including craftsmen and service providers) aware of the special situation of the field workers so that we don't feel that out of sight is out of mind.

There is another solution, which we are not interested in: for us to become more *autarkic*, a kind of "agricultural farm" owned by the kibbutz. We consider ourselves an integral part of the kibbutz and want very much for the present split to be eliminated.

These problems, raised by Yoash's stories, troubled us for a long time after he left. We thought about what we could do, discussed the issues at our kibbutz meetings, which we held every Saturday evening at the doors to our rooms, and tossed out a great many ideas that led nowhere.

When Yoash read us poems, he was different, as if he were singing, not reading. On those evenings, he brought us actual books—by Ayin Hillel, Leah Goldberg or Oded Burla—and his dramatic voice became lighter and happier. Of the poems he read to us, our favorite was Oded Burla's "We picked meadow flowers today."

> We picked meadow flowers today,
> Liron and Tamir and I.
> Liron picked tall stalks,
> I chased after locusts,
> And Tamir called out: Look what I picked!
>
> We rode the train yesterday,
> Liron and Tamir and I.
> Liron counted bridges,
> While I read a book,
> And Tamir asked: Who's driving the train?

And on it went until Yoash read the last line: "And Tamir drew a scribble," which made us think about the scribbles of the Anemone kids, who were a grade below us in the Children's Society, and the childish, illogical things they did, and we laughed and laughed, then went back to thinking about all that until we fell asleep.

5

Kibbutz Yehiam stands on an isolated hill at the foot of a Crusader fortress whose beauty can be seen from far and wide.

In his book *1967*, Tom Segev describes the founding of our kibbutz, Kibbutz Yehiam, quoting from the diary kept by Yosef Weitz, a leader of the Jewish National Fund, whose son, Yehiam, was killed in a Palmach operation in 1946:

> Three months after the Night of the Bridges, Yosef Weitz traveled to the Arab village of 'Zib, north of Acre, and from a distance observed the place where Yehiam had been killed. "I couldn't go right there and prostrate myself and search for the drops of blood which the earth had soaked up," he wrote.

Looking east, he saw the remnants of Qala'at Djedin, or the Heroes' Fortress, an impressively tall stone tower built by the Crusaders that had become a stronghold of the Galilee ruler Daher el'Omar. The sun was setting, the tower "glimmered and lit up the entire area, all the way to Haifa." And then Weitz knew; he swore that this would be where Yehiam's monument would rise. A new Jewish pioneering settlement had to be built here, in this place, for defense, for forestation, and for agriculture. "The fortress shall be renewed and it shall be ours," he wrote, "and above it shall fly the name of Yehiam, a token of innocence and dedication and sacrifice, and by its side an eternal flame shall send light into the distance." This endeavor, Weitz told his wife, Ruhama, would be their solace. Thus Kibbutz Yehiam was founded.

Every Independence Day eve, we stood on the lawn in front of the dining hall in the U-shaped formation that allowed everyone to see everyone else, and we all wore white shirts with *yizkor* (memorial) pins that had a picture of the Red Everlasting flower on them. Gilad gave the signal with his trumpet from the dining hall roof, where he stood near the flag that had been flying at half mast for Memorial Day and then raised for Independence Day. On the lawn below, a bass voice cried out: "Kibbutz, attention!" And then: "Kibbutz, at ease!" Then we all went up to the fortress along a path lined with torches.

Standing in the large open area beneath the fortress, we raised our heads to look up into the sea of flames. Words made up of huge letters that had been strung along iron wires were set aflame. Every year, we were surprised once again by the fireworks that lit up the sky, some of which were made from weapons and grenades that had been collected all year, developed and improved especially for that night.

The entire history of the fortress, from the time of the Crusaders in the twelfth century to the Independence Day battles, was written on the blue Nature and Parks Authority placards placed in front of the fortress and inside it.

Our silo, the silo of a Hashomer Hatzair kibbutz, and yes, our pigsty, were built at the foot of the fortress, similar to the way the Christians or Muslims, in a newly conquered land, build a church or mosque near an older church of a different denomination, or on the ruins of a mosque they have vanquished. But the Crusader fortress remained standing under the sky, on the top of the hill, looking out over the entire breadth of the landscape, its existence revealing history—a beautiful, imposing presence that continued to exist in parallel to our own religion, which was aimed at creating a future different from anything humanity had ever known before, and destroying the past.

The members took advantage of every opportunity to tell themselves and us the story of how the kibbutz was built. Sometimes they danced or sang it, sometimes they sat on the stage and recounted it to one and all. As if the story about us, that we told to ourselves all the time, on kibbutz holidays, on quiet evenings, in newsletters, in letters, in end-of-year plays, expanded our brief history, thickening it, justifying it, adding meaning to our existence.

We loved the plays and songs more than the reality of our daily lives, but if they lectured the history to us, we didn't understand a thing. The events didn't seem to connect to each other. The continuity was broken. We couldn't connect the Holocaust with the War of Independence, and with the fact that it all happened to our parents. When exactly, where exactly. They showed us the places in the fortress where they had been entrenched, and the scorched bullet holes.

The story that the old-timers loved to tell the most, as if they had to tell it, was about the early days of the kibbutz. They told it to us on Saturdays, or when they were at work or walking through the fortress with us. They told it to each other on kibbutz holidays and in newsletters.

It began in Kiryat Haim, where the old-timers lived in May '46. There were about ninety members, most of them in their twenties, on a plot of land that had a single building and tents on it. They were called Kibbutz Hasela ("the rock") then.

Hasela consisted of two totally different core groups: the Meadow group of the Israeli movement, and the First of May group, made up of former members of the Hashomer Hatzair movement from Hungary and Slovakia.

As was customary in all Hashomer Hatzair kibbutzim, while the members were preparing to settle in their permanent home, they worked outside the kibbutz: in the port, in the Naaman factory, in the Mivreshet factory, in bourgeois city homes as cleaners and laundresses, and doing any other odd jobs they could find that would earn money for the kibbutz.

Later on, everything happened quickly: the members of the various groups still hadn't had time to bridge the huge gaps between them—they included former members of the Hashomer Hatzair group of Rehovot and the Ben Shemen boarding school, as well as the Hungarians and the Slovakians, who had arrived only a few months earlier from the hell of World War II. They were six months into their year-long training period, learning to cohere into a well-functioning group, when senior delegates from the Kibbutz Artzi Economic and Settlement Committee arrived at Kibbutz Hasela in Kiryat Haim with news: they would have to move to a new destination and settle there urgently.

The new destination—Djedin—was surprising, as was the urgency of the move. The Kibbutz Artzi spokesmen said that they would not paint a pretty picture of their new home: none of what they needed to survive could be found in Djedin. There was no water, no land, no food, no weapons, no way to support themselves there. It was a true wilderness in the heart of a hostile population.

They said they knew that the groups had not been together long enough to cohere into a true kibbutz. They said that there were severe problems with the water supply to that particular point, that under such conditions the army should be posted there, at the foot of a fortress with no land, but a Hashomer Hatzair kibbutz was preferable to any military unit. And the more time they spent describing the overwhelming difficulties and the beauty of the fortress, the more attached the members grew to the place, even before they saw it. After the kibbutz held marathon discussions, during which Avraham Herzfeld, Yaakov Hazan and Yosef Weitz spoke, a decision was taken to move to Yehiam, which still bore the name of the ancient fortress, Djedin. At week's end, a large majority of the members of Kibbutz Hasela voted in favor of the Kibbutz Artzi proposal: an urgent move to Djedin in the Western Galilee.

It was decided that the children and most of the women would remain in Kiryat Haim, in Kibbutz Hasela, until basic conditions for housing had been established at the foot of the fortress.

On November 27, 1946, only one week after those marathon discussions, the men climbed up to Djedin, carrying all their equipment on their backs.

The members of Hasela changed the name of the kibbutz to Yehiam, after Yehiam Weitz.

Everyone in the Yishuv (the Jewish population of Israel prior to the establishment of the state) knew of the Weitz family. Yosef Weitz was one of the heads of the Jewish National Fund and had been involved in establishing many settlements, including kibbutzim in the Western Galilee and the Jerusalem neighborhood of Beit Hakerem, where he lived with his family.

On Yehiam, we called him the father of the kibbutz. The old-timers sent him radishes, packed in a shoebox, from the first crop planted at the foot of the fortress, and we, the Narcissus children, celebrated his eightieth birthday, the very same year we celebrated our tenth. It was then that our teacher taught us the meaning of the word *gevurot*, which literally means "strength" or "might," but has come to represent anyone who reaches the age of eighty.

If "aristocracy" hadn't been such an ignominious term in Hashomer Hatzair, Yehiam Weitz, Yosef Weitz's son, could be called the personification of the Eretz Israeli aristocracy. He was the son of parents who came from prominent families (Weitz, on his father's side, Altschuler on his mother's), and the brother of Professor Raanan Weitz, one of the leaders of the settlement movement and the Chairman of the Jewish Agency Settlement Department.

Yehiam was born in Yavniel, grew up in Beit Hakerem, attended the Gymnasia Ivrit in Rehavia, and was a member of the Hashomer

Hatzair youth movement. He worked in Kibbutz Mishmar Haemek before he left for the University of London to study botany and chemistry. He graduated with honors and was accepted by the Hebrew University in Jerusalem. When World War II broke out, he left his studies and, as one of the first company commanders of the Palmach, became one of the models for the iconic image of the Palmach soldier.

In 1946, on the night between June 16th and 17th, the Night of the Bridges operation was carried out, in which Palmach units went out to blow up eleven iron bridges, roads and train tracks at eight locations in the country, in order to cut off the access of troops from neighboring countries. Yehiam Weitz's unit came under attack by Arabs guarding the bridges. He was the first to be hit, and died immediately, while the other thirteen soldiers were killed when bullets hit the explosive materials they were carrying and the railway bridge collapsed on them after they took shelter between its columns.

He was twenty-eight when he was killed, married to the singer Rema Samsonov. No one had been named Yehiam before him. Many, including Kibbutz Yehiam itself, were called Yehiam after him.

Tom Segev describes his extraordinary funeral:

He was buried just as he had lived, as the son of his father, a prominent figure in a very small society: almost everyone knew everyone and many were related. "Jewish Jerusalem in their thousands yesterday accompanied Yehiam, the son of Yosef Weitz, to his final resting place," reported the daily newspaper *Davar*. The national flag was draped over the body. Thirteen men had been killed with Yehiam that night, but their bodies had been shattered, thus his funeral stood for theirs, too. The public was called to take part: in Haifa, where the funeral procession began, all work came to a halt, transportation stood still, schools were closed, In Jerusalem, the procession could hardly make its way through the crowds. Yehiam was buried on the Mount of Olives.

The newspapers continued to follow avidly the heroic story of the Yehiam settlers, and Rafael, a member of Yehiam's Meadow group wrote in his diary:

> When we arrived in Yehiam, we divided the kibbutz into two: one part, in Yehiam, consists mainly of men, and is a proud place that stars in the newspapers, a mecca, where all hardships are endured with love. The other part is in Kiryat Haim. Mainly women. They work at odd jobs, earn money for the kibbutz, take care of the few children and yearn for the day they can come to Yehiam.

Yehiam did not have a battle tradition; we were not forced to know about the battles it had fought, nor did we learn its history in an organized manner. We tried to listen again each time it was mentioned because we wanted to know, but we never understood. Sometimes, we felt that, for a brief moment, we had suddenly grasped what preceded what, but over and over again, we lost hold of that understanding. It was as if it sank into the fortress cisterns, like the stone used to demonstrate gravitational force for us: it fell and fell until it landed on the bottom of the cistern with the dull sound we waited for expectantly so we could estimate the depth.

Zvi Gershon and Natan Flesh told us that in the beginning, the members who came to Yehiam lived in the fortress. The water they managed to collect in its ancient cisterns was brown, moldy, and rife with mosquito eggs. In order to purify it for drinking, Natan Flesh poured airplane fuel into the cisterns and ignited it. Sometimes, if they used the wrong amount of fuel, all the drinking water, sparse to begin with, was lost. Sometimes the members lost consciousness, one after the other, when they went down into the ancient cisterns to clean them.

There was no other water, neither in the fortress cisterns nor anywhere else on the kibbutz land. Transporting it was difficult and complicated, and it was done on the backs of donkeys. A member would send a Morse code signal from the top of the fortress to Kiryat Haim, where the rest of the members were, telling them how much water to bring. Then they would calculate how many people were

Kibbutz members cleaning old water cisterns in the fortress.

needed to carry the container from the van, which could come only as far as Hagaaton Valley, but couldn't remain there for long because of the gunfire. From there, they had to carry everything on foot, and every day, they had to deal with the question of how many people there were to carry it all on their backs, and how many donkeys would have to help them.

They told us that the kibbutz was isolated and cut off, and the road leading to it hadn't been paved yet. Cars drove to Hagaaton Valley, and people, donkeys and mules walked from the valley to Yehiam along an overgrown path that became negotiable because of constant use. In winter, on rainy days, walking required great effort. The split between Kiryat Haim and Yehiam separated families, members, friends and even the members of various committees. The two parts of the kibbutz communicated through signals sent mainly at night. There was a machine in Yehiam that threw shafts of light to a distance of forty kilometers, but only if the weather was calm and the air bright and clear, with no rain or fog. Morse code was used to communicate, and generating the electric current needed to signal was complicated. They used car batteries, which they had to charge every few weeks. That was how they sent their regards, personal messages and requests for supplies. Coded messages regarding security matters were sent on wireless radios.

At 1:30 AM on November 29, 1947, one year and two days after the first members arrived at Yehiam, the signal station in the fortress received a telegram from Kibbutz Hasela in Kiryat Haim:

Long live the Hebrew state.
And Yehiam replied:

*Sela from Yehiam: Mazal tov to you from the Arab state. Have
a goodnight.*

From that night on, as a result of the partition plan adopted by
the United Nations General Assembly, the borders of the Hebrew
state had been drawn south of Acre (on the banks of the Naaman),
and Yehiam was therefore inside the Arab state.

Tom Segev writes in *1967*:

> At the end of 1947, war broke out. It resulted in the establish-
> ment of the State of Israel, and its territory included Yehiam
> as well as West Jerusalem and other areas not intended for it
> under the partition plan. Yosef Weitz believed that the suc-
> cess of the Zionist enterprise necessitated the removal of the
> Arab population from Palestine. During and after the war, he
> was involved in deporting Arabs from territories conquered
> by the IDF, preventing refugees from returning, and forcibly
> transferring Arabs within the state. In the 1950s he was in-
> strumental in attempts to encourage Israeli Arabs to leave the
> country. He continued to believe in the "transfer" of Arabs to
> the end of his days.

Every now and then, we went up to the fortress, and one of the
old-timers would retell the story of the War of Independence battles
for us or someone else he was showing around, and bits and pieces of
what he said stayed in our minds. Sometimes, we managed to grab
hold of the beginning of the plot, other times it melted in our ears as
soon as we heard it, or it was only the end that we grasped. The cisterns, the malaria, the shooting; in which convoy had the members
been killed, the one to Yehiam or the one to Keziv; was it an attack

At the outpost during the Independence War, 1948.

on Yehiam, or in the Auschwitz camps. One convoy merged with another; an armored vehicle with a train.

Zvi Gershon, who was chosen from the members of Yehiam to be commander, ordered all the others to sleep with their shoes on and guns cocked from that night on. He told us that everyone knew it was only a matter of time before Yehiam—a small, isolated, mountain settlement accessed by only a single road that wound through Arab villages—would come under attack. Blowing up one bridge over the Gaaton River would be enough to cut it off.

About a month and a half after the night of the Partition, on January 11, 1948, Yosef Weitz wrote in his diary:

> From the morning on, I met with representatives of the settlements in the area. I am especially concerned for Yehiam. The sparse rainfall has not brought water to the cisterns, and

to this day, the members endanger themselves by transporting water from Nahariya. It is essential to level and pave the road, which will require a budget of 15,000 liras. And more buildings and work are needed. They are isolated and alone. Can they endure? And for what? This question troubles me from time to time, shaking the unshakeable view I held before the United Nations decision that it is good for us to have agricultural settlements in the Arab state. Has there been a weakening in my faith that the day is approaching when the Western Galilee will be ours? For without that faith, there is no point in sacrificing and investing. I would like to do something for this place, but I fear the objections of others. Especially of the Settlement Department. And the young men here are so nice and good, and they never hesitate.

Nine days later came the attack that surprised everyone with its intensity: At dawn on January 20, 1948, the kibbutz was attacked by a regiment of the Arab Liberation Army, under the supreme command of Qawuqji. Troops from neighboring Arab countries had been mobilized into that regiment by Adib Shishkali in Lebanon. The attack raged for six hours, as the regiment attempted to invade and conquer Yehiam.

During the attack, the bridge over the Gaaton River was blown up. Yehiam was inundated by rifle, machine gun and mortar fire for the entire six hours.

From Tree Hill, where we used to take walks almost every week with Rivka, our teacher, the members of Yehiam recognized Adib Shishkali, the well-known military leader, who later became the president of Syria. He sat astride a white horse, commanding his troops. That attack on Yehiam, the first one of such magnitude in the War of Independence, is considered an extraordinary one to this very day. The attacking army was repulsed after many of its number were killed and wounded. In Yehiam, four were killed and six wounded. Also killed were six guards traveling in the armored van that accompanied the water transport to Yehiam. It came under attack on the road and burned.

Zvi Gershon said that, in addition to attempts to airdrop supplies to the kibbutz from light planes, a supply convoy was occasionally sent from the coast.

On March 27, 1948, one such convoy, an especially large one that included ninety soldiers, set out from Nahariya on its way to Yehiam. Halfway there, it was ambushed by the people of the adjacent village, al-Kabri.

In Yehiam, they heard the noise and saw the columns of smoke, but did not know what was happening. Nor did they know exactly how many people there were in the convoy and which members of the kibbutz had joined it. (Members who had managed to get away from the kibbutz to arrange things and organize supplies, or those who were coming from Kiryat Haim for a short visit, always joined the convoy because that was their only way of getting to and from Yehiam.)

Zvi Gerson relates that the first armored vehicle, fitted with a barricade breaker, reached Yehiam. There were fourteen fighters inside it, including the company commander, Eitan Zeid, who was killed, the severely wounded armored vehicle driver, and another wounded man. The fighters who managed to reach the kibbutz didn't know how the rest of the convoy was faring. Neither coded nor uncoded communications reached the members in Yehiam with further information about the fate of the people who were in the other vehicles.

Forty-seven of the fighters and passengers in the convoy were killed. The old-timers always said that, of all the terrible nights Yehiam had experienced, that one was the worst.

After the convoy was wiped out, Yehiam came under total siege. A large number of all the weapons in the entire Western Galilee had been destroyed in the convoy, and no one knew how long the supplies and arms in Yehiam would last.

In a letter written by Avri Sela on April 2nd, less than a week after the convoy disaster, he described the situation in Yehiam: the failed attempts to prepare a landing strip that would make airdrops of food easier; the endless barrages of bullets being fired at them; the shortage of weapons and their feeling of apprehension in the face of Qawuqji's large army, which was concentrated on Tree Hill, 1,452 meters from the fortress. He wrote about the bereavement:

> Shall I write to you about our mood? It must surely be clear to you. There's Haim Drori, the soul of the kibbutz, work scheduler, purchase coordinator, janitor, alert to everything going on in the kibbutz. He was so alive before that it's difficult for me to talk about our lives without complaining that Haim didn't do this or that the way it should be done. And Laki—only three weeks ago he came with the new car, smiling as usual. He was so good, so devoted. And Rafael, tall, wild Rafael, always writing. Such a deep thinker. We have lost three dear members in a single day. It is difficult to imagine life without them.

Two days later, on April 4th, Qawuqji's troops attacked Yehiam again. They opened fire just as the plane was dropping supplies and kept at it for several hours, but made no attempt to invade the kibbutz.

Shosh Shoresh, the wireless operator and one of the few women in Yehiam during the war, said that it wasn't until Tarshicha and the Western Galilee were conquered in the Hiram Operation on October 30, 1948, that the war in Yehiam ended. On that day, she sent the last two telegrams to Nahariya: "At 7:05, the white flag was raised on the Tarshicha mosque," and "I'm closing the station until further notice."

When we were in the third grade, every Tuesday evening we would sit in our classroom with Hencha, who brought stenciled songbooks with her and taught us the songs in them. On those evenings, we didn't sing about the Budyonny Regiment riding into battle, but we sang slower, sadder songs, like "The Fisherman's Daughter." We also learned new words from the song "aflutter" and "incomparable."

An airplane dropping supplies for Yehiam,
when it was under siege by Arab fighters.

Hencha would occasionally stop the singing and tell us about the first children on the kibbutz. She was those children's first *metapelet*, back when the kibbutz was still in Kiryat Haim and was called Hasela. She told us that one of the things that set the kibbutz apart from its very beginning was the fact that it had children older than the kibbutz itself. And the four of them were allocated a place in the only building on the plot of land in Kiryat Haim that the members had at their disposal at the time. The first group of children was called The Rock (Hasela), the same name as the kibbutz when it was founded, before it was changed to Yehiam.

She told us that when the War of Independence ended, they began the actual work of building the kibbutz from the ground up. The siege and the gunfire had almost completely prevented them from building the kibbutz during the war, and after it, they continued with the rock demolition up in Yehiam, in search of water sources.

All of that took almost a year, during which the women and children remained in Kiryat Haim. When you are building a kibbutz, a year is an eternity, Hencha said. For the women who stayed down below in the Kirya, it was the very worst time. Their numbers decreased, every day something else was dismantled and someone else went up to Yehiam, and only they stayed behind. They couldn't take part in building the kibbutz, and had to make do with hearing reports and an occasional visit.

They were so sick of it, she said. They didn't even have a kitchen anymore and had to eat at Kibbutz Hahotrim, whose members lived on the adjacent plot of land. It was as if they belonged to that kibbutz, not Yehiam, and they couldn't have any social interaction of their own there.

The first farmer and plow in Yehiam, protected by an armed guard.

One day in early June, 1949, a taxi arrived at the Kirya, and Eliezer got out of it and ran straight to the chicks that were waiting there to be transported up to Yehiam. But Hencha had had enough; she was angry that everything and everyone else came before the children, even the chickens, as if no one up there in the fortress even remembered that they had children. That was after she had warned them again and again that the women were about to come with the children, and no one had listened to her.

She told Eliezer that the taxi would take the children to Yehiam and his chicks could wait. She snatched the taxi right out from under him. They arrived and announced—we're here. No one was waiting for them in Yehiam, and nothing was ready. But despite the difficulties, or maybe because of them, Hencha said, the *metaplot*, the members and the children were very happy that they were all together again after the long, two-and-a-half-year separation that began when the members first went up to Yehiam and the kibbutz was divided into two.

On June 12th, one week after Hencha and the children left Kiryat Haim, the first baby was born on Yehiam itself. That was Ofer, my oldest brother, and my mother said on one of the kibbutz celebrations, or in the fiftieth anniversary film, that everyone was ecstatic. Like in fairy tales, my parents' little shack seemed to be covered with sweets and goodies. And that was my mother's most intense experience of togetherness, of how it is possible to fully share a joyful experience.

Filled with happiness, everyone rushed to their house to congratulate them. Ofer was in the Grove group, the kibbutz's second group.

When the winter of the children's first year in Yehiam arrived at the end of 1949, Hencha thought that they might actually have made a serious mistake by taking them there. They couldn't do anything

The first children on the Yehiam kibbutz,
with the Crusader fortress in the background.

with the children that winter. The entire kibbutz consisted of a small tin shed that housed the metalworking workshop and another shed where the carpentry workshop was, near the fortress, and the bakery. Everyone lived in small sheds like the shoemaking workshop, and the rain leaked in. You couldn't wash clothes or dry out shoes. There were no paths or sidewalks, and there was a great deal of mud. The rain didn't let up for two weeks.

Hencha sometimes told us about the children who were on Yehiam when it first began, and then we'd go back to singing. The evening we learned "The Fisherman's Daughter" was especially cold, and frightening claps of thunder boomed right above us. We were so deeply immersed in Hencha's stories of the first children, the harsh winter of the kibbutz's early days, and the new song we were learning that when we started singing again, the mountain farm blended with the seashore of the fisherman's daughter. Even after Hencha said goodnight, closed the door and left, we kept on singing the new song we'd just learned, as if it were a prayer:

> Across the water a fisherman sailed
> Out to the deep sea afar
> A gray-eyed young maiden stood watching
> And sent out a prayer from her heart
>
> Dear Lord, watch over the ocean
> And safeguard the watery ways
> For like me, boys and girls stand ashore
> And fishermen's children are they
>
> Into the distance the fisherman vanished

The wind gusted over the water
Back on land in the darkness she stood
All aflutter, the fisherman's daughter

Dear Lord, watch over the ocean
And safeguard the watery ways
For like me, boys and girls stand ashore
And fishermen's children are they

Back to land did the fisherman row
From wave to wave with his oar
While she, the incomparable maiden,
Still whispered to sea from shore

Dear Lord, watch over the ocean
And safeguard the watery ways
For like me, boys and girls stand ashore
And fishermen's children are they

—Lyrics by Binyamin Avigal, music by Miriam Avigal

6

Onward to Yehiam, hey hey hey
Every night and every day—Yehiam (2X)
We'll rejoice, rejoice, rejoice in Yehiam
We'll rejoice, rejoice, rejoice in Yehiam.
Onward to Yehiam, hey hey hey.
Every night and every day Yehiam. (2X)

The song was preceded by a countdown from ten to one, which some-times began at the quarry junction and sometimes on the Gaaton turn-off. We don't remember who counted or gave the signal to start the countdown that preceded the song. We weren't strictly observant about the kibbutz anthem; we didn't even call it that. If there was a countdown—we sang. If there wasn't—we continued to sing canons that had no special meaning and went on forever, like, "Hey, a long and winding way, green grass and weeds the live long day. (Second voice): Li lo li lo lay, green grass and weeds the live long day."

We rode in a GMC back and forth to doctors in Nahariya or to Yehiam's fields in the Kabri Valley, bouncing along in the hope that the moment we were called to work would be delayed, that the ear-nose-and-throat doctor in the Nahariya clinic would get in the way of a Katyusha rocket before we arrived. We stared at the most mysterious sign of our childhood, which stated: "Please Do Not Throw Out/Cigarettes and Matches in the Pail." Each of us wracked our brains trying to find an answer to the riddle: How could the sentence be punctuated to avoid contradictions, and could it possibly be suggesting that cigarettes and matches should be thrown outside and not inside the pail? And where was the pail anyway?

The song about Yehiam wasn't a typical kibbutz song. It didn't have any particular choreography to go with it, or even a real melody. We kind of recited it, with the "hey hey hey" coming out of nowhere, the way it does in a shepherd's song. As if whoever wrote it had spent only half a day on it, then had gone back to work in the fields.

Every few years, Yaakov R. was reelected kibbutz secretary, and when he held the office, he gave a speech and made a toast on Rosh Hashana and Passover. His holiday speeches were filled with the mention of crops, as were all the secretaries' speeches, but they always had an undertone of subtle sarcasm, a sort of second voice like the one in the two-part harmony sung by the choir that was waiting to perform when he finished. "*L'Haim*, comrades," the secretary said loudly, raising his eyes from the pages of crop statistics and waving his glass in the air, after he'd described how the bananas had been pounded by a barrage of hailstones and the avocados had been killed by frost. The "*L'haim*, comrades" was repeated a moment later, after he described the political reversal that left us, the political left, without a hope. And so it went, one blow after another, until he raised his glass again, and in a bitter voice totally unsuited to his holiday toast, repeated the words as if they were the chorus of a lament: "*L'haim*, comrades."

Yaakov R.'s sarcasm and irony expressed neither despair nor scorn. They were part of the efforts he made to illuminate the various issues he raised. Yaakov had unique control over his words: He would juggle his arguments in the air, twist them around when they were up there, stop them for a moment in mid-air so the entire kibbutz could stand beneath them and see their other side, then he'd lower them slowly until they landed on the ground.

Since he was a man of action who also knew how to speak more eloquently than anyone else on the kibbutz (his speech wasn't flowery, but rather almost lyrical), he'd been elected right from the beginning, as if out of nowhere, to lead, to formulate that leadership. He was the one who wrote and read aloud the Djedin scroll, in which the kibbutz members had sworn a blood oath to the place, at night, before they began their climb to Yehiam. Later, he represented the kibbutz in its dealings with the various institutions. During the War of Independence and the siege of Yehiam, he risked life and limb on his many urgent trips to Haifa, Tel Aviv, Jerusalem. He had to find a way to supply Yehiam with everything it didn't have—land, food, water, ammunition, ways of earning money, cigarettes, and everything necessary to life.

During a fateful kibbutz meeting that took place during the war, on May 15, 1948, when the kibbutz was still split between Kiryat Haim and Yehiam, Yaakov posed the question that had been hovering over Yehiam from the moment it was created on a rocky, isolated hill, and later, when the Partition map placed it inside the borders of the Arab state, and it was engaged in heavy fighting and under ongoing siege:

Is there any chance that we can live in that place, he asked? And who should man the forward post—the kibbutz or the army?

The actual issue under discussion was whether they should stay or leave Yehiam. "Our purpose," Yaakov said, "is the purpose of every kibbutz, first and foremost to become a cohesive group and prepare ourselves to build a functioning settlement. I asked the powers that be why they don't take us out of Yehiam. All the answers were only strategic. They do not see us as a settlement, but rather as a position that will defend the Western Galilee. And we cannot take risks. The military knows that only a kibbutz, not army troops alone, can hold the place. They did not tell us what the political considerations of the Kibbutz Ha'artzi are, so I am not sure that the Kibbutz Ha'artzi can go to the institutions with such a demand, but that should be our purpose."

At the end of that discussion, it was decided that Yaakov and Abush would tell the powers that be, including Yosef Weitz, what had been discussed and what was happening in the kibbutz.

On May 18, 1948, three days after that discussion on the kibbutz, Yosef Weitz wrote in his diary:

> The Western Galilee was liberated yesterday, after we took all of Acre, but the problem of Yehiam has yet to be solved.

Abush and Yaakov, members of Yehiam, came to see me. The mood there is very dark: Very little food, water is sparse, the place is under fire by snipers almost day and night. All the airdropped items do not reach them, only about a third or a quarter, and the people there ask: What is it all for? If Yehiam is in the Arab state, then it will not be built, and why have people given their lives? And our country's leaders say over and over again that we will not take more than the United Nations has allocated us. I found it difficult to give them an answer, since I do not share our leaders' view. We must conquer the entire Western Galilee, for we have shed blood over it. But I agree that the members should leave, and if the commander considers it important militarily, he should send army people there and not rely on settlers. This must be clarified with the Haifa commander.

I am enclosing pages from Yediot, published by the secretariat of the Kibbutz Ha'artzi Hashomer Hatzair, in which there is a description of the attack on Yehiam. The writer is also no longer among the living...

He was referring to the piece written by Rafael, of the Meadow group, about the first attack on Yehiam in January 1948. Rafael was killed two months later, in March, in the Yehiam convoy.

When the war ended, the kibbutz received land in Gaaton Valley and Kabri Valley. At noon, all the members gathered for a meeting with the settlement and Kibbutz Haartzi institutions. The question was, once again, whether to leave the kibbutz, only this time, they discussed the issue from the civilian, agricultural settlement point of view: Should the kibbutz be moved closer to its new lands, or remain where it was, at the foot of the fortress in Djedin-Yehiam, where there was almost no agricultural land?

During the discussion, opposing views, both emotional and practical, were voiced. All the speakers said that so many near and dear ones had sacrificed their lives so the others could live in this place. "How can we leave now?" they asked at the meeting.

In the end, the majority of the members voted in favor of keeping the kibbutz where it was. They didn't want to leave because of the beauty and wildness of the place, because of the living and the dead, and so the fields remained separate and far away from the kibbutz.

The separation between the fields and the kibbutz that was created in Yehiam was extremely unusual in the structure and agricultural-social-economic concept of kibbutzim. Based on that concept, the link and proximity to the fields were at the very heart of the kibbutz vision of the new, productive, creative man. Work was not a means or a tool for personal profit; it was perceived as an entity in and of itself, and a source of interest and renewal.

The geographical conditions of a mountain kibbutz cut people off from their fields, as if a mountain and a valley of hardships have been placed between them and the work they do.

Though the physical distance between Yehiam and its fields created economic and transportation problems, it did not adversely affect the connection between the members and the fields. As in all kibbutzim, the fields were the focal point of our conscience and everything we reported about ourselves revolved around them. They were the place where records were constantly being broken.

The first paved road to the kibbutz,
a cause for celebration because work could begin.

Nothing interrupted the old-timers' work, not quotas that were already filled, not holidays or Saturdays, not even children or rest. As if they were in a huge, boundless laboratory of space and time, they immersed themselves in work and saw the fruit of their labors come to life in the growth of the kibbutz.

Dov P. said the early years of establishing banana growing as a profitable branch of the kibbutz, from the time he completed his training in 1954, were the happiest years of his life. At night, he waited for morning to come; he had no patience for the night, which interrupted everything, and he would get up and smoke (or smoke and get up) and think about the bananas in the valley, about what each member of his crew would do. Fifteen or eighteen sweaty, drenched members picked thirty tons of bananas in the rain. The record was seventy tons on a single Saturday. They came home dog-tired, but happy. Within four or five years, Yehiam had the largest banana plantation in the area.

The old-timers were happy in their work. Their reward was their work, and vice versa. We all eagerly followed the yield much the way you follow a drama taking place right in front of your eyes. Breaking agricultural work records was the only possible compensation. There were no salaries or other material benefits. The reward was sweeter than anything material; it was sweet, like art, like the joy of doing for its own sake, as its own reward, like a harvest, like an annona or a banana picked straight from the tree.

New records for each season were reported in the newsletter: For example, the season's largest cluster of bananas (42 kilograms); the average weight of largest clusters to the end of February (24.3 kilograms).

Harvesting bananas.

New inventions, improvements and innovations in agriculture were most highly praised, since they combined several greatly valued principles: creativity, productivity, and industriousness. Zvi Gershon, along with Yoskeh, invented weapons during the siege. (They made mines and bombs with a pliers, a screwdriver and a hammer. With the additional help of a hand drill, they produced dozens of explosive devices that they spread along the fences, and land mines that they buried on the roads leading to Yehiam.) After the war, Zvi Gershon continued to devise agricultural innovations that increased production. For example, he discovered that by dragging four corn seeders hooked up to the back of a tractor, seeding capacity could be doubled. The newsletter said that people flocked from all the agricultural settlements in the area to see the innovation and copy it for themselves.

Thanks to the hybridization carried out by Yair Argaman in the orchards, the entire country's production record for miniature fruit trees was doubled. "Two and a half years after he planted the miniature orchard, we were producing two tons of fruit per *dunam*[7] of land, which is double the normal crop in Israel for trees that age. A crop that size in this kind of orchard is a national record."

The newsletter said that scientists, instructors and fruit growers from the four corners of the country came to see that achievement with their own eyes.

Yaakov R. and Yehuda Harari thought about work all the time, even when the working day was over. They thought about it as they walked, hands clasped behind their backs, as if their bodies had

---

7 A unit of land measurement in Israel equal to 1000 square meters.

twisted physically into questions and thoughts, and now they were thinking back and forth, plowing their thoughts.

Even in the children's houses, when they came for fifteen minutes to tell us bedtime stories before we went to sleep, if they had an idea, they would pace in the corridor, or even in the room itself, which was only about four meters long. They would pace, stop, turn, then start pacing again. They thought about work, became immersed in their thoughts about it, contemplated various ideas, problems and solutions.

Yaakov R. was the most eloquent speaker on the kibbutz. He didn't use flowery words, but rather words of action, of persuasion. However, since he was a man of work, he had an occasional attack of hatred toward his own powers of persuasion and refused to speak. And then, like the tug-of-war game played on the Shavuot holiday, the entire kibbutz moved to the other side of the rope and fought Yaakov to make him speak. That's how it was from the beginning, at the kibbutz meeting on May 20, 1947, which discussed the road-paving holiday. The kibbutz was still split, and the members up in Yehiam wanted to celebrate a great holiday—the paving of a section of the road to Yehiam. The following was said at the meeting:

> "We've come up against the problem of the speech to be given at the celebration. The fact that Yaakov is going away for a seminar doesn't change anything. He can come back for two days to be at the party. Yaakov told the secretariat that he was opposed, and now he has to convince the kibbutz."

Yaakov stood up at the meeting and said:

> "I cannot say anything at that celebration because I have

nothing to say. Giving a speech is, in some ways, like art. Just as a person cannot write a poem simply because someone has decided that he must, so it is that I cannot give a speech at this celebration."

The decision: To compel Yaakov to speak.

In favor—20. Against—5.

The magic of Yaakov's speeches did not carry over to his writing; nor was he one of the people on the kibbutz who wrote manifestoes, aspired to be a Knesset member or anything else that would utilize his skills. His art lay in his ability to formulate the relationship with the community; his art was bound up with action. When he spoke about something, we could see the various sides of yes and no as if they were the sides of a cube. He once said to us:

There was only a superficial understanding of the individual-collective dichotomy. The idea was actually that the individual was very important, and it was believed that the more devoted the individual was and the more he did for the community, the more he would develop.

That was the philosophy, and we accepted it totally. There were always some members who did not contribute very much to the collective—we, who contributed, felt much happier, much more complete, much more satisfied than they did. And to a great extent, we were. They were bitter, and we felt that we were building a world. That is to say, it was not a matter of the individual sacrificing for the collective, but rather it was a matter of the individual developing through the collective.

Later, Yaakov said:

There can be no doubt that this perception has not stood the test of reality, the test of time, and today, it is anachronistic. We must not return to it.

He always contradicted what he'd said, or blunted it, as if he'd packed his perception into a suitcase, and now others had to come along and offer their merchandise. He needed other proposals in order to practice his powers of persuasion.

Yaakov's words caused us to go back and forth from thought to reality. When they hit their target, they were like the agricultural innovations—setting new records of reality—or like Ari's matchstick models.

Ari had a special status. He wasn't one of the old-timers; he wasn't an original core group member, nor had he been added to one later. He was born in the kibbutz, a child in Grove, the kibbutz's second group, and our groupmate Zohar's older brother. Since he was twelve the newsletter had been reporting on his handiwork the way it reported on the orchard and banana crops. Ari knew how to build anything with matchsticks. The entire kibbutz eagerly followed the new records he set, which he himself broke every year. The new model was exhibited on the kibbutz holiday. In 1963, after the seventeenth one, the newsletter reported:

Without any doubt, Ari's matchstick creations—the Eiffel Tower, the railroad train, the ship bridge—were the greatest attraction. In order to give an idea of the amount of work he invested in them, suffice it to say that the ship was made of 37,280 matches glued together, which is almost 980 boxes.

Later on, Ari made exact models of the kibbutz houses and the silo.

When we, the kibbutz members, stood in front of Ari's scale models, which were displayed on tables, and leaned toward them to see every detail better, we were overwhelmed by the sheer number of them. Sometimes forgetting that they were only models, we entered and walked around in them in our minds, and when we remembered that we had to return to reality—we suddenly froze in place with fear. For a moment, everything was topsy-turvy: We were afraid that the kibbutz itself was only a scale model of something much larger, whose creation had snagged in the middle, and that in fact, all our work was in vain, no one was walking behind us to expand the kibbutz enterprise, and what we heard was the sound of our own work shoes clacking on the stone sidewalk. We were afraid that our kibbutzim, like Ari's scale models, like buildings we'd constructed with temporary beams, were only decoration, the physical embodiment of Yaakov R.'s arguments, an image. As if all the kibbutzim were meant from the beginning to be only the setting for puppets that had escaped from a puppet show and were wandering everywhere on the kibbutz, in the cow barn and the animal pens.

Ari's models filled us with a strange intoxication, just as Yaakov's speeches did, as if both were ladders on which we climbed from reality to the rarified air of the loftiest peaks where records were so phenomenal that they verged on fantasy, and for a moment, we were able to live inside the tower of the dream of justice, equality and truth that we had built in the air.

7

Thanks to the fortress and the hill, Yehiam was saved from the low-ceilinged, uniform decor of the kibbutzim. The steep inclines made bicycle riding impossible, and boredom did not overlay it like fog.

The natural setting of Yehiam was wild and colorful, as if the buildings had been dropped into a nature reserve below the fortress. The kibbutz was rampant with flowers, bushes, trees, grass, rock gardens, soil enriched by pine needles, and there were brown, green, yellow, pink and white corners everywhere. Different flowers bloomed every season, and trees lost their leaves or filled with green.

When darkness fell, the volunteers looked up at the sky, enchanted. They explained that in the cities they came from, the buildings and lights hid the sky, so they didn't know, or had forgotten, that there were so many stars. They lay on the lawn in front of the dining hall and in the open area in front of the fortress, their faces tilted up to the sky to better see the Milky Way.

The darkness around the kibbutz was a totally black, but non-material presence. You could walk through it, shorten the distance from one place to another. The stars shed their light from the sky, and on the ground—the fireflies. The chicken coop workers wrote on the bulletin board: "If you're interested in the coop and what we do in it, and also want to see a festival of animals at night, you're invited to see deer, wild boars, snakes and jackals."

After work, the volunteers sat at the pool, in the fortress, in the clubhouse or on the dining hall lawn and wrote long, long letters to their families, covering thin stationary paper with their rounded handwriting. They described the Crusader fortress for them, and the Milky Way, the weeping willow that stood on the lawn near the swimming pool, the Judas tree at the entrance to the kibbutz, the brightly colored oranges they'd picked at noon that day, the jackals and the wild boars.

We walked on the stone sidewalk. We collected acorns from under the oak trees to use their bases as candleholders for the crooked Hanukkah menorahs we made. As we walked, we turned over stones to see earthworms crawling on the pine needles.

We were never able to comprehend what Yehiam had been before, that there had been nothing here but the fortress, nothing. Twenty years ago, it was all barren.

The fortress and the land around it was purchased in 1938, eight years before the kibbutz was built on it. The people of the northern district of the Jewish National Fund bought it in the internal competition they had going with the southern district. The land was very problematic because it was not arable. It was all rocks. The beauty of the fortress was of no use as far as building a settlement was concerned. In his book *From the Edge of the East* and *Deep in the Heart,* Mordechai Shachevitz wrote:

> It consisted of 3,342 *dunams* of rocky land of unimaginably hostile wildness. Only fifty or sixty *dunams* of it were workable, most of it around the fortress, and only a very small bit of land west of it, in the middle of the craggy area.
>
> This land was bought, despite the fact that it was totally unsuitable for a settlement, because of the competition between those involved in land purchase: The people in charge in the north wanted to prove to [Yosef] Weitz that what Yoav could do in the south, they could also do in the north. [...]
>
> The land was purchased from a Christian Arab named Hawa, father of the poet Ramonda Tawil [and grandfather of Suha Arafat], who was very active in the war the Palestinians fought against us. How the land came into his possession, God only knows. His forefathers apparently received it from the Turks in one of the weird ways those things were done in the last century, and if they paid for it at all, it was most certainly a very small amount. [...]
>
> A Bedouin tribe, the Arab as-Suweitat, lived mainly in the small western part of this land and grew tobacco. The purchase agreement called for them to leave, and though they had already received the compensation that was coming to them, they refused to go and hoped that their intransigence

would be rewarded with compensation a second time.

The members spoke about Israel Caspi, the kibbutz's first gardener, as if they were speaking about a miracle that happened, without mentioning the forbidden word, miracle (because miracles occur independently of man, ex nihilo, and on the kibbutz, we believed in cause and effect, in man and his actions, which is why the word vision was always used). They said that his visions could not be believed. Because what he saw was so extravagant. Almost imaginary.

Anywhere else in Israel, the members said (maybe when Yoash told us about a mountain kibbutz, maybe they told each other about it on the stage on one of the kibbutz holidays), you could simply plant grass, flowers and trees. But Yehiam, which was excellent as a fortified military post on an isolated hill, provided nothing a settlement needed to survive. Everything had to be brought from the valley: earth, water, food, ammunition (to survive in the face of enemy

Clearing the ground of stones and rocks to make way for the Yehiam fields.

gunfire and to use for blowing up the rocks and preparing the land).

The sound of dynamite, which was always used to blow up the rocks in Yehiam so that the land could be used for planting, accompanied by a warning cry, which was shouted loudly before every explosion, could be heard many years after we were born. Yehiam was built on rocky land. Preparing every *dunam* for agricultural use required hundreds of days of tenacious, backbreaking work: exploding the rocks, removing the broken pieces and building gradients. The second stage was the transport of soil from the valley, and only after that could grass, flowers and trees be planted. It took hours of grueling work and enormous sums of money to build each house. In order to plant the lawn in front of the dining hall, for example, more than two hundred truckloads of earth were brought from the valley.

Those who worked with Israel Caspi said that he had a mental image of what the vegetation, sidewalks and rock gardens of the kibbutz should look like. An image of everything that was not there. And it led him to become an expert in all things that stood in the way of his vision: paving walkways, cutting paths, building fences. He became a construction expert, an experienced tractor driver (including heavy equipment), and a plumber.

Since he wanted to preserve the natural landscape as much as possible, he built the sidewalks from the local stone, not cement. He used local rocks to create natural rock gardens. He brought Judas trees—which painted the entire kibbutz purple—from the *wadi* and planted them in Yehiam, and like a painter, he searched the nearby natural environment for all the other colors he'd seen in his mind and brought them to Yehiam for planting.

When the War of Independence ended, he pruned the withered

branches of the oak bushes, which had been gnawed at by goats and were completely flat and gathering dust on the dining hall lawn (of course, there was no lawn or dining hall yet). He said that those bushes would grow into beautiful oak trees. You can't believe him, the members said. As the years went by, the kibbutz filled with trees, some of which he had uncovered and pruned, and others he had planted: decorative trees and wild trees, elms, pines, cypresses and others beside the oaks and terebinths that had grown from pathetic, faded bushes into dark-foliaged trees. In the early days of the kibbutz, everything had been exposed and arid—you could see the distant countryside and the sea from everywhere on Yehiam—and suddenly, you had to go up to the fortress to see above the treetops that covered everything with dense, thick vegetation.

During those early years between 1949 and 1951, Yosef Zaritsky painted his famous watercolor series, "Yehiam," from the fortress on Yehiam. His abstract paintings perfectly depicted the idea of ex nihilo creation.

A ceremony laying the cornerstone for the first brick building in Yehiam, 1950.

Winter was the most beautiful season on Yehiam. The clouds and the lightning hung low over our heads, and the rain gushed down the narrow stone sidewalks. No one picked the cyclamens, narcissi or anemones that carpeted the kibbutz like brightly colored lawns.

Stories of Israel Caspi's deeds were told outside of Yehiam, and this is what the *Al Hamishmar* newspaper wrote about him in 1952:

> A significant experiment in methods of mountain foresta-
> tion, whose results might have far-reaching effects for years
> to come—was done by Israel Caspi, a young forester on
> Kibbutz Yehiam in the Galilee. His method is based on the
> Lysenko method used to forest the steppes of the Soviet
> Union, and consists mainly of planting dense "nests" of oak
> and other tree seeds in larger quantities than has been usual
> in Israel. Some of the seeds fuse with others because of their
> close proximity, and with their joint strength, grow into
> healthy and robust seedlings. This new method is still in its
> inception, and according to Israel, years of experimentation
> are still necessary to draw final conclusions. What is already
> clear, however, is that the pace of growth is faster, which will
> allow for a more rapid development of natural groves.

Trofim Denisovich Lysenko, a Soviet biologist whose name and teachings had so many legends associated with them in those years, was later denounced as a ruthless dictator in Stalin's service. Lysenko claimed that it was possible to ignore the history and genetics of plants and create "a new plant," to intervene in the heredity of plants and engineer them to have new traits. By the early 1960s, his crimes had already been exposed, crimes against both the scientists who objected to his teachings—in response, he shipped them off to death camps and had them executed—and against science, when it turned out that all of his claims were blatant lies and brazen manipulation. The supposed scientific proofs were a cruel farce.

But Israel Caspi succeeded, with his own hands, in transforming even Lysenko's scientific lies into truthful facts in Yehiam's natural environment.

Israel Caspi was Yehiam's first "landscapist," long before Yoash came to us from Kibbutz Palmachim for ideological reasons. He was one of the Poles who, like the Hungarians, arrived after the war. We didn't know him; he died before we were born. They said he was perfect—handsome and smart. He shot himself to death in 1953 after his girlfriend was killed on an excursion to Petra. There was no point in planting a tree, or even an entire forest, in his name because all of Yehiam's glorious beauty—the natural rock gardens, the lovely narrow sidewalks, the wild cyclamens, the thick grass, the brightly blooming trees—was his vision and his soul, which blossom and wither and blossom again with all the seasons of the year.

8

The founders of our kibbutz consisted of two main groups: the "Israelis" and the "Hungarians."

Later came the "French," the "South Americans," and individuals or small groups from many other countries.

Apart from their different native countries and languages, the old-timers were different from each other in many other ways, and we didn't know how they managed to get along. The adults lived their lives on a separate planet from ours.

The founders—the Israeli Meadow group and the Hungarian First of May group—first laid eyes on the rocky ground of Yehiam in 1946. The Israelis knew the language well, not just Hebrew, but the language of the land, of hiking trails, of the Israeli holidays. Back then, Zimi (from Hungary) wrote this:

When we discuss our approaching *aliyah*[8] to join the kibbutz, Hebrew words appear here and there, but our main language remains Hungarian. And like our knowledge of the language of Israel, such is our knowledge of the realistic conditions.

We have only vague notions about everything. Those who came to organize us warn us again and again: the land apportioned to you is especially rough. You'll find mostly rocks there, but no water [...] They ask us to get out and cover the last part of our journey...on foot. At that moment, we feel what it will be like on Yehiam. Everything is crumbling, both inside us and in the countryside. Rock-strewn hills, a horizon of dust and sparse bushes. Absolutely nothing. All the way to the place where we will have to put down roots. The Israelis, who have more direct contact with the life here, consider coming here a heroic act in a hostile environment. It is true that everything is sublime here. But right now—I don't feel very enthusiastic.

The members of the Hungarian Workers group were not among the kibbutz founders. They joined Yehiam after the War of Independence, in 1948, after a year of training in Kibbutz Sha'ar HaAmakim and after the Israeli Meadow group and the Hungarian First of May group had already internalized the rules about Hebrew that were customary in Hashomer Hatzair kibbutzim.

Members of The First of May locked Hungarian away in their hearts. They read only Hebrew books. And they so internalized the

---

8 The common name used to describe both an immigrant to Israel and the waves of immigration by Jews to Palestine and later Israel (i.e. the First *Aliyah*, the Second *Aliyah*).

Hebrew regime that they spoke only Hebrew to each other. So did our parents. The only sentence in Hungarian that we sometimes heard in our biological homes during our afternoon visits to our parents was made up of two words that flew over our heads: "*Hoi diod*," which means, "Let it go," the short version of, "Come on, it doesn't matter. Don't fight with the child when he's only here for an hour and fifty minutes."

But members of the Workers group had a different attitude towards the obliteration of Hungarian. At bedtime in our room in the Narcissus group, Shlomit whispered (tenderly) to Ronen: "*Chilagom*," "*Daragom*" (my star, my dear one). The rest of the parents spoke Hebrew like *sabras*[9] or had been speaking Hebrew with a Hungarian accent, but grammatically correct and without any terms of affection. When Shlomit and Edna (from the Workers group) were on night shift in the children's house, they sometimes left us French fries, which for us were like a Hungarian lullaby. (Food not at mealtime, and food that was merely a treat, were categorically forbidden.) They put them in a bowl on the counter in our dining room, sometimes adding a letter: "To the Narcissus children, goodnight to you, from the night shift." Once they even drew a moon on the bottom of the letter. Those nights were our happiest. After the French fries we found on the counter, our dreams became as light as a white cloud, like a holiday.

The members of the Workers sometimes clapped their hands together, glanced up at the sky, sighed and said, "*Ishtenam burzulom*— "Dear God!" (And not only did God not exist in Hashomer Hatzair, but he was forbidden; he was an irrational, pagan obstacle to the

---

9 A nickname for native Israeli Jews, taken from the name of a common cactus in Israel.

remarkable abilities and productivity of the sublime human being. God was a vestige of the dark Middle Ages, held in even greater contempt than Hungarian or tender words and lullabies.)

On Yehiam, where we grew up, we spoke correct Hebrew and pronounced names properly. We didn't know that during their first years on the kibbutz, the old-timers had warned and reprimanded the Workers over and over again on bulletin boards and in the kibbutz newsletter about speaking Hungarian:

> Language is a major problem in your absorption into our kibbutz. In our last newsletter, we mentioned the effect of language on our children. Things have reached a point where a mother speaks Hungarian to her son. You must show your willingness and make an effort to restrain yourselves from speaking anything but Hebrew.
>
> I have a request to make of you: please, speak Hebrew at least in public places! The Kibbutz Movement has always prided itself on the fact that new immigrants on kibbutzim learn to speak Hebrew quickly. The dining room and everywhere else is buzzing with Hungarian. Even the kitchen is run entirely in Hungarian.
>
> Not all of us are "Hebrews." A large number of us come from abroad. We too came to a Hebrew community. We didn't know Hebrew, but we were still ashamed to speak a language other than Hebrew in the dining room, and if we didn't know how, we kept silent or at least whispered if that was the case.
>
> If you begin speaking Hebrew in public places, you will get used to the language and speak it in your rooms, too!

The kitchen buzzed with Hungarian, as the notice on the bulletin board said, because the kitchen workers sat on low stools peeling potatoes with no rotation in sight, and the women who cooked in enormous pots stood on their feet and never sat down.

When we, the Narcissus group, passed through the kitchen as part of our "help the *metapelet*" program, the workers called us over for a minute, quickly, so no one would see or hear them pampering us, and let us taste the food. And they also asked us if it was good, fishing for compliments because there were no compliments on our kibbutz. Applause at the end of a performance was frowned upon too; that was a bourgeois custom.

The women who worked in the kitchen and were rebuked for speaking Hungarian preferred to stay close to the food. They had been starving when they came from Europe and took greater pleasure in soup and bread than in people, whether they were socialists or not, whether they spoke Hebrew, French or Hungarian.

We thought that all the Hungarians in the world were older. All the ones we knew were older. And there was also a minority of parents from there who had survived and were even older than they were: grandparents. They were called Grandpa Vilmosch, Grandma Guttman, and so on. All the Hungarians were our parents, and the smallest minority, a handful of survivors, were their parents.

Only once did we see a Hungarian girl our age. She was Idit's cousin, who came for a surprise visit one summer. She wore an embroidered white blouse just like the blouses sent to us in packages from abroad that we would open and send straight to the *communa*, so they could be turned into travel clothes for all the children and come back to us, too, when it was our turn to go to the kibbutz apartment on Sheinkin Street in Tel Aviv once every summer with our biological families.

The embroidered white blouse she was wearing was hers alone. She ate every meal with us around the small Formica tables and went to the pool with us every day. She was so pretty. The Hungarian she spoke sounded like a mistake to us, the standard deviation of a single case.

It wasn't only language that separated the Hungarians from the French and the Israelis. The French were more talkative. They hadn't come in a single large group after a bitter war that left them no choice, as the Hungarians had, but had made *aliyah* in organized groups of various ideological persuasions during the '60s and '70s after freely choosing to leave their homes and jobs in Paris and move to a place where they believed that everyone was working to fulfill a dream, but came up against the kibbutz. They wanted to establish a new, progressive society. As they saw it, they had been hurled to the ground and they believed that the Israelis, mainly the Hungarians, were the killers of their dreams.

The Hungarians said that, for the French, work clothes were merely a costume, while the French said that there was nothing worse than listening to a stupid Hungarian who thinks he's smart.

The French sometimes wrote open letters in the kibbutz newsletter before they left. For example, in 1977, they wrote:

> We had to be more than a little crazy to take ourselves out of a life that was organized (according to well-planned steps leading to a brilliant career) in the leftist style of the Jewish students in Paris, as well as in every other place in the Diaspora.
>
> But the true test of our ideas has come.

With eyes closed, as if in a fog, we made *aliyah* to a kibbutz. All of you more or less know the rest of the story.

We had the feeling that the people asked themselves: what are these guys looking for here? A year passed and a few members of our group (out of twelve) decided that true realism is in the Diaspora.

Two years passed and another few left for all kinds of reasons, and with a bitter taste in their mouths.

Three years have passed, and the last remaining members are trying to find their way in this country. I take the liberty of mentioning these facts because of the sincerity of this experiment.

[...] Regarding the French group of Kibbutz Yehiam, I can now say that the experiment is ending in total failure.

Our group has not been assimilated into the kibbutz. There has been no integration between us, as "Jews from France," and you, as Jews from Eastern Europe, the earliest members of the kibbutz and the young sabras, because of a mutual lack of communication and understanding.

And so, an entire French group left. Other French members remained.

Smoking on Yehiam was like an additional language. In addition to their faith, each in his own way, in a better world to come, the Hungarians and the French were also united by their profound love of cigarettes.

But again there were disagreements about all things related to the manner of smoking.

Hungarian smoking had no breaks, hesitations, rules or rests; it was work, and it seemed to come in place of speaking, a part of what they were working at.

The term "passive smoking" didn't exist in those days, but if it had, it couldn't have applied to the Hungarians and their children. We loved cigarette smoke and never waved our hands around to disperse it.

In our biological home, we were already allowed to smoke on Purim when we were in the first grade. When we were in the fifth grade, and still on Purim, our parents told us in our biological family—my three older brothers and me: "We know you'll smoke. Obviously you'll smoke your first cigarette with friends, but the second one you'll smoke at home; don't hide it." They kept repeating that as if they were sitting impatiently on the edge of the couch, anxious to get past that inevitable moment, the moment we'd start smoking. The four of us really did smoke. The windows in our parents' house were never opened when we were smoking.

When a relative or friend of the Hungarians died, the death announcements were sometimes passed from one to the other in the following form: "Zili has stopped smoking." And there were no misunderstandings. No Hungarian ever stopped smoking in those years unless he was dead.

Hungarians never put their head back when they're smoking, and they don't exhale slowly and luxuriously. They seem to only inhale, never exhale. The argument about whether to inhale or not could take place only in America, never in Hungary.

The inhaling was deep and full of longing—longing for the next puff, that is, the next cigarette that was on its way right now and would lead to the next pack. Because they inhaled so deeply and for so long, Hungarians would smoke a cigarette in two-thirds or, in some cases, even half the time it would take other smokers, whether they were French, Israeli, South American or anything else.

Hungarian smoking had other striking characteristics apart from its intensity: there was no place where smoking was inappropriate, and going from one place to another did not mean taking a break from smoking. On the contrary. After all, it was a waste of time not to smoke when you have to go somewhere. And the expression "cigarette break" had no meaning for them because they had no breaks from work, or from anything else, and also because they smoked constantly and continuously, lighting one cigarette with the butt of another.

Already during the first kibbutz meetings in November 1946, the Israelis pleaded to issue regulations about smoking restrictions in various places, including during the meetings themselves. The Hungarians objected firmly to regulating or restricting smoking in any way. When the Israelis asked for smoking to be permitted only in open areas, at least, my father said, as recorded in the minutes: "No one has ever died from smoking, but millions have died from the cold."

For fifty-six years, a file was left sealed in the Yehiam archives: Yaakov Carmi's file. He was killed in January 1948, in the War of Independence, during the first, fierce attack on Yehiam, which also killed three others. He was buried under his name, but no one knew his true identity or his family. People on the kibbutz had barely gotten the chance to get to know him because he was killed a very short time after he came there.

In 2004, a man arrived suddenly from Tel Aviv asking for details about him. The only thing the old-timers could recall after straining their memories to provide a few answers for the man who had been searching for him for fifty-six years, was that he had been older than most of them and even a worse chain smoker than the other Hungarian chain smokers. His archived file contained only one letter he had received from his sister in Hungary ten days before he was killed. There was no address on it.

To the man from Tel Aviv who was searching for him, they gave the letter that had been left in the file, the letter that had come for the Hungarian smoker whom no one on Yehiam had a chance to get to know, the letter that came such a short time after he arrived on Kibbutz Yehiam from the war in Hungary, and ten days before he was killed on the southern post of the fortress, by a mortar shell in a battle that went on for six straight hours.

During the long siege of Yehiam, the members sent the other half of the kibbutz (which was still in Kiryat Haim with the children) Morse code messages listing the supplies they needed.

After the list of vital supplies was decoded, they were airdropped from the skies over Yehiam. Ezer Weizman was one of the pilots who airdropped those supplies. Every day, a flashlight signaled the Kirya: "Send cigarettes urgently." Sometimes, the joy after the airdrops turned into annoyance and disappointment, like on the day the plane rained candy over Yehiam, but no cigarettes. That evening, they learned that a mistake in deciphering the Morse code message had led to the bitter substitution of candy for cigarettes because in Hebrew, the words are so similar (candy is *sucariot* and cigarettes is *sigariot*).

Two weeks before the disaster of the convoy that was attacked on the way to Yehiam in March 1948, the members trapped in the fortress had completely run out of cigarettes. When the war ended, the commander there, Zvi Gershon, wrote about that:

I don't smoke. But for some reason, I had collected about two hundred cigarettes. I used that stockpile to help the smokers who were suffering the most, handing out half a cigarette a day. As members of Hashomer Hatzair, many of us didn't smoke, and we were shocked to see how desperately the smokers needed a cigarette.

The lack of cigarettes made them jumpy, and they launched a search for something they could smoke. They foraged for butts that had been tossed casually away during times of "plenty." Investigation revealed that the members who were staying inside in the sheds flicked their cigarette butts through the window at the stone fences that enclosed the small buildings. That was a very significant discovery. They immediately took apart the fences, pulled out the cigarette butts, removed the little tobacco that was left, rolled new cigarettes and smoked to their heart's content.

When the plane appeared overhead, the smokers would look at it, breathless with anticipation. I remember one of the professional smokers running after the parachute and opening it, and when he saw that it contained only bread, he kicked it furiously.

That was when I began using my hidden treasure of cigarettes to encourage people to go out on patrol. I gave out "prizes"—half a cigarette before patrol and half afterwards. The smokers would fight over the right to go out on patrol... And they also tried to find substitutes—smoking dry leaves. My Morse code messages and demands to send cigarettes were to no avail, and the people suffered terribly.

Some of us asked ourselves if the day would ever come again when a member could tap his comrade on the shoulder and say simply, "Give me a cigarette."

Zvi Gershon, who was both wartime commander on Yehiam and the inventor of agricultural machines and techniques in peacetime, hit the nail on the head in describing the professional smokers.

Because with all that the Hungarian smokers had in common, they fell into different categories. The categories of smokers cut across lines dividing urban from rural, members of The First of May from member of the Workers, touching only on the number of cigarettes the smokers consumed. Papa, my mother, Agi, Esther N., Yuda B. were all in the same category: heavy, not fussy Hungarian smokers who went through about three packs a day. They weren't choosy about the kind of cigarette, and even if they did prefer a particular brand, they always smoked what was available. One cigarette was stuck in their mouth and another waited its turn behind their ear or in their hand, or had been placed on a chair beside them. They lit the cigarettes with matches, not lighters. There were also more stylized Hungarian smokers, but only for the sacrosanct purpose of making people laugh, and they would exhale the smoke through their ears, like Zambo.

The very best, in a league all their own, were the Szandors. Flawless professionals. The Szandors were master craftsmen of smoking. All the ash of their cigarettes remained hanging in one piece and never broke in the middle. The phrase "flick your ashes" had no meaning for them.

Even while they were still alive, we called cigarette ash "szandor" in their honor, saying things like "Don't drop your szandor on the

Zvi Gershon on a "camel," an agriculture machine that
he invented for collecting tobacco leaves.

floor, here's a szandortray." He was very tall, an ever-present stock-
ing cap on his head, and she was very small. The identical way they
smoked made it seem as if there were many more than two of them,
as if they were an entire troupe and not just a couple.

Miriam Szandor, in addition to her regular job, ironed and
folded laundry for soldiers on Saturdays. And even when both hands
were full of work, the eternal cigarette was stuck in her mouth.
Avraham Szandor had the same smoking technique. The cigarettes in
their mouths never went out, not even for a second, as they did for
every other smoker. And they inhaled constantly. We used to watch
them as if they were magicians. Even when our eyes were glued to
them and we concentrated, we never managed to see the moment
when they switched from one cigarette to another.

The only time Szandor's szandor fell was when the famous shot
blasted into the Szandors' room. A stray bullet flew through one

window and out the other, and they say it hit Szandor's szandor on the way, but apart from that, nothing happened. Inquiries were made, however, about who fired the shot and why. But about the fact that there had been a stray bullet, there was no disagreement. The matter was closed.

Perhaps because of the art of smoking that characterized Yehiam, the most popular branch on the kibbutz was tobacco.

When they first began growing tobacco, in 1953, it was part of the vegetable garden, which is why it was located on the kibbutz itself and not far away in the fields. That was still before they established the prestigious and productive branches: the citrus groves and the bananas.

Drying tobacco leaves.

The beginning was very difficult; the tobacco wasn't planted properly and mistakes were made in the drying sheds. Diuri, from the Hungarian Workers group, who was in charge of the tobacco growing, thought they should dry the first-year leaves in an open area and close down the tobacco branch. But supervisors from the industrial department of the Agriculture Ministry said that the tobacco plants in Yehiam were uncommonly beautiful and convinced him to continue. After a period of trial and error, Yehiam became the only kibbutz to succeed in growing Virginia tobacco. Kibbutzim that tried to grow it in other areas failed. For a variety of reasons related to the quality of the soil and its salinity, the tobacco that grew there did not burn when put to the test.

Our tobacco world was shrouded in magic and mystery. Its stars were the planting fields, the "camel," a machine two-and-a-half meters high invented by Zvi Gershon for spraying and picking tobacco—and rituals that included tying the tobacco leaves on long poles and climbing the walls of the drying sheds to hang them. When the drying sheds were opened, the aroma of tobacco spread throughout the kibbutz like Hungarian perfume.

With the years, the Virginia tobacco grown on Yehiam made an excellent name for itself and Zerah Gahal, the national tobacco king from Dubek, the city cigarette factory, would sometimes come to the kibbutz, smell the tobacco, stroke the leaves, impressed by its quality.

The parents and children of the members, the *mossadnikim*, volunteers and group members worked with tobacco. It was everyone's favorite place to work. On days when there were fierce hailstorms and the workers couldn't go out into the fields, they came to help sort and pack tobacco leaves in the sheds.

The tobacco branch closed down in 1971 and we, the Narcissus children, grew up in the shadow of the closing and never had the chance to work there. When we passed the old-timers walking up or down the narrow and steep stone sidewalks, we said hello to all of them. That's what we were taught—a kind of bourgeois-European custom that had survived the New Child regulations.

When we bumped into Diuri, our groupmate Hagit's father, we knew that they said he had never recovered from the kibbutz meeting where it had been decided to stop growing tobacco, which despite the certificates of excellence it received every year, was no longer profitable. Since the tobacco branch had been closed down, Diuri's gentle smile was marred by a small cloud of sadness that went with him everywhere, like a column of smoke. When we met him on the sidewalks, we saw the tobacco sheds in our mind's eye.

We said good morning or good evening to him and nodded in mute condolence. After all, we were children and couldn't vote at the kibbutz meeting to overturn the decision to stop growing tobacco.

Leaving sadness behind, we ran down to the field to play prisoners or dodge ball, or up to the reservoir pool to sail on the rafts we'd built for ourselves from boards.

9

There were four of us, my three older brothers and me. The first family in Yehiam to have four children.

We came to see our parents at 5:30 and went back to the children's houses at 7:20, Ofer to the Grove group, Yochai to Pomegranate, Yair to Pine, I to Narcissus.

None of the four of us ever ran away to our parents' house at night, as so many of the other children did. Maybe we were afraid they'd send us back, or maybe we were afraid they wouldn't. The children who did run away were humiliated and bitter every time their parents returned them. To reach their parents' house, they had to cross the entire kibbutz in the dark, in the middle of the night, in the cold and rain. And they were sent back immediately.

We didn't even try. In our recurring dreams, Nazis marched down the lovely narrow stone sidewalks, passed the reservoir, skirted Abrashka and Rachel's house at the beginning of the row, and went into our biological parents' house. Then we would wake up.

We slept in our parents' house only two or three times during our childhood. For example, in the sixth grade, when kids, exactly our age, with names just like ours, came from other Hashomer Hatzair kibbutzim and slept in our beds as part of what was known as "the hospitality program." The hospitality program, which lasted for three days, was a substitute for the religious-urban-bourgeois bar mitzvah, which was never mentioned in our kibbutz. It was a kind of coming-of-age journey. We boarded Egged busses, excitedly paid for our tickets and rode for several hours in groups of four children, with no adults, until we reached another part of the country. The scenery might have changed, but the trip brought us to a place very similar to our own. Our group went to Reshafim. Other groups, to Mishmar Hanegev and Beit Alfa. For three days, we lived their lives with them, which were identical to ours. We went to class with them, worked with them on their children's farm instead of our own, and returned on an Egged bus.

Several weeks later, when four children from Kibbutz Reshafim arrived in Yehiam for three days, we gave them our beds, which were identical to theirs, and the heavy yellow bedspreads, and slept in our parents' house, a strange and terrifying sleep. Our parents' close proximity seemed sick and crazy, as if we were locked in an embrace with death, which sang us a lullaby. We could hardly wait for morning to come.

Most of the Narcissus children had older, Hungarian parents.

The entire Neeman family in Yehiam: the oldest son,
Ofer, sitting first on the right, second child Yohai sitting on the left,
third child Yair standing behind the parents. Yael is sitting on her mother's lap.

We never had anyone from outside the kibbutz in our group. Every night from the time we were brought from the hospital, we slept surrounded by walls covered with yellow oil-paint. The aesthetics of the children's houses, if the word aesthetics can be used in connection with such an ugly place, were based on the absence of color and stimulation. That was part of the system. Four children to a room, two boys and two girls. One in each of the four corners, a nightstand beside each bed. The ugliness didn't bother us. We overcame it with the gold of our imagination.

The *metapelet* said goodnight at 9:30 every night, after she finished reading us a new chapter from *People of the Beginning*, by Eliezer Shmueli, about the guards who rode their noble steeds, or a chapter from *The Adventures of Neznaika and his Friends*, who flew around the whole world in air balloons. "Goodnight," we replied, waited for her to close the door behind her, and got up. We couldn't sleep.

In the hot summer, we dipped our sheets in cold water, shouted "We're Greeks" at one another, and ran down the corridor in dripping togas that cooled our bodies. If the mosquitoes bit us, we went into the *metapelet*'s room and put together a concoction that we thought would soothe the bites. One of us was always on guard duty, keeping an eye on the sidewalk that led to Narcissus to warn us if the night guard was coming. If she was, we'd jump into our beds, turn our faces to the wall and pretend to be asleep, trying not to laugh at Moshik's histrionic snoring. The night guard left after less than half a minute, hurrying off to Terebinth or Anemone. Bye and hope not to see you again. We got up again. Sometimes we didn't have enough time to jump back into bed, and the night guards would catch us and give us a good talking to. We didn't get upset because there were different night guards every week, and we were permanent. They didn't know anything about children's sleep habits at night. We didn't know anything about theirs.

My three older brothers and I were like guests in our parents' house. Our parents didn't know what size shoe we wore, and when I asked for wooden clogs with a blue stripe for my tenth birthday, they bought me a pair that was three sizes too large. When the clogs finally arrived after having been changed, I ran back to the children's house at 7:20. The new clogs could be heard from far away, clacking happily on all the stone sidewalks. I had to take them off at the door to Narcissus. They were too private and the stripe was too blue. "We have sandals that Pirosh made in the shoemaking workshop for all the children" (carrot-orange for the girls, brown for the boys), the *metapelet* said.

We never told our parents stories like the one about the demise of the clogs, maybe because we didn't want to sadden them. We, adults and children, lived in parallel universes, each universe with its own problems, each with its own difficulties. You don't burden children with adults' tears or Holocaust nightmares, and vice versa. We didn't tell them anything. We said: the words will never pass our lips. Our parents didn't know anything about our lives and we didn't know anything about theirs. Maybe the *metaplot* rebuked our parents about the clogs, maybe not. We didn't know. We too wanted to maintain equality and didn't understand exactly how we had forgotten and had dared to ask for our own clogs with a blue stripe.

(The following item appeared in the newsletter, under the head-line "The Problem of Sharing and Equality Among the Children": The kibbutz provides all clothing and footwear, without exception—including house slippers, or white wool. Therefore, no one should have personal items such as clothing, sandals, *kaffiyahs*, etc.)

Our parents apparently never noticed the series of deer names in our biological family: Zvi (deer), my father's name; Ofer (fawn), my oldest brother's name; and Yael (ibex), my name. Otherwise, they wouldn't have disrupted it with Yochai and Yair, the non-deer names of my two middle brothers. There were other families on Yehiam who had children with a series of thematic names, such as Hadas (myrtle), Vered (rose) and Nitzan (bud). Or Netzer (shoot), Rotem (broom plant), Erez (cedar) and Oren (pine). Nature, of course.

But there were no animals or plants in our biological home, which was headed by two urban people: my mother, from Budapest, in Hungary, and my father, from Torna, also in Hungary, and Vienna, in Austria.

For years, they made do with a hose and a few roses, which hinted at a garden and gardening, and hid the shame of their non-existent garden. (Gardens beautified the entire kibbutz, not only a member's house, and an untended garden therefore made the entire kibbutz ugly.) Sometimes, our parents asked us to help them weed or water the garden. Abrashka, our neighbor who lived in the last house on the street, helped them figure out what needed to be uprooted, that is, to differentiate between decorative plants and weeds. He also put his tools at their disposal.

Every few years, they enlarged the paved area a little bit more. Their houses are called "Ein Dor houses," after the architectural style that was conceived in Kibbutz Reshafim, but came into its own in Kibbutz Ein Dor. The old-timers' neighborhood in Ein Dor is called Tel Amal (after the houses in the Tel Amal settlement, which later became Kibbutz Nir David). Each kibbutz added improvements and developments, and contrary to stars or plants that are sometimes given the names of the people who discovered them, the buildings in a kibbutz were named after the kibbutz from which the latest model arrived. Kibbutz architecture did not center on the architects or the buildings, but rather on man and his needs.

Nature was never discussed in our biological home. On kibbutz marches or hikes, when we trudged along after the explanations given by Eliezer A., a mushroom expert, we talked about other things and didn't notice when everyone stopped beside some rare mushroom.

We only had to really pick flowers in the garden once a year: six flowers on Holocaust Day.

We would stand in the doorways of our parents' houses when the siren sounded, and listen to Yoash's voice reading the text about the six million, which came through the invisible loudspeaker on the dining hall roof and echoed throughout the kibbutz, as if it were coming from the sky or from hell.

We—Anat, Hagar, Amos and I—stood in the doors of our parents' houses, ready to go into action. It was always the youngest child in every family who had to pick six flowers at the end of the ceremony, in memory of the six million Jews who perished in the Holocaust. We didn't know what our parents were thinking, whether it was about their families who'd remained there, or not, about the homes they'd had there, or not, about the Danube, which my mother said froze over in winter, or about our dry Gaaton River.

When the signal for our choreography, picking the six flowers, was given, we all ran into Abrashka's garden, which was filled with gerberas, tulips, red and white roses. The other gardens didn't always have six flowers in them. Eli Harari, who also cultivated his garden on the other side of our house, focused more on trees—lumquats and pomegranates—and less on flowers.

After we brought the six gerberas or roses or tulips, according to the tradition established by the Kibbutz Artzi national committee for holidays and ceremonies, but adapted by the culture committee of each kibbutz to suit its needs or local holidays—our parents were supposed to tell us about the Holocaust.

In a kind of balance of terror, we would release each other after a few minutes; the story would be told on a different occasion, "After all, we don't have to do this just because it's Holocaust Day," my mother said every year. Before we took off through the door or the window (we moved the screen and jumped), we tried to remind our parents to put the six flowers we'd picked, the gerberas or roses, in water. But they didn't always do it. Just as they didn't always take the things we brought from the children's house and hang them up or collect them. In fact, they never did.

When we brought a carving we made from an avocado pit, our parents would throw it into the garbage pail without the slightest hesitation. "It'll get black anyway," they said, either to us or themselves, we couldn't be sure, then dropped the lid over it. Sometimes, before the sentence was carried out, we tried to argue that it was a key holder or a bookmark, not just an ornament, that it was something practical they could put to use. Our parents viewed with suspicion and an obvious lack of affection everything we made and brought them at 5:30 from the children's house: Hanukkah menorahs made with acorn bottoms; bookmarks made from dry red leaves; crooked clay vases. In our house, we knew that none of us was a plastic artist and nothing we made was of any value. Sentimental value was, of course, out of the question—we had no concept of it or words to describe it. In rare cases, usually when words, poems or other sorts of writing, never drawings, were involved, the items were collected and put in the attic. Our parents couldn't climb up there anymore, and we were in charge of it, determining who was chosen based on changing criteria set by a different brother each time, to go up and bring things down.

Only we knew what was up there, and in what order, and we would throw things down when requested—blankets, pillows, folding beds, Ofer's poems, a file of letters that had been forgotten there, and then, in a different season, we would wrap the winter blankets and heaters in plastic and return them. "Is everything organized up there?" "Can you get through?" were the questions our parents asked from down below, because for years they hadn't had any idea of what was happening up there. "It looks great here," we said from above, "everything's organized and clean. One look, and you can see what's here. Don't worry," we said, and tossed down a piqué blanket they'd asked for. Then we climbed down on the slats of the wooden shutter we used as a ladder.

In our biological home, time was measured by the glass clock made by Gila, my mother's cousin, who had lived across the hall from them in the apartment house in Budapest. We loved Gila and Pishta, her husband, and all the glass things they made for us: a nameplate for the door, a table for the living room, jars, clocks and more. They had studied in Italy after the war, and the glass that Pishta blew always reminded us of the glass slipper and the ball. When the hands of the glass clock reached 7:20, we went back to the children's houses. Sometimes, our parents would be busy with their committees or work, and my brothers would tell them, "Okay, we'll walk Yuli to Narcissus." My middle brother Yochai had given me the name Yuli when I was still in kindergarten, and ever since, that's what everyone on Yehiam called me. I loved the name Yochai had made up for me, and I loved my three brothers more than anything else in the world. (Ofer was older than I was by eleven years, Yochai by six, Yair by five.)

We felt like guests in our parents' house, and we never interrupted each other with questions like: Did you really say that to him, or did you just think about saying it? Just the opposite. We felt obligated to include as facts all the things we thought about saying but didn't. And every time we retold a story, we embellished it even more. If we didn't embellish or change it, we couldn't retell it because

the listeners or we ourselves would be bored. My brother Yoachai
kept the rules, and sanctified our right to exaggerate.

We exaggerated so much that I thought Leah Goldberg wrote
her poem, "Chan-So-Lin," about us. I believed that because the
poem is about three older brothers and a younger sister who wanted
golden slippers and velvet slippers:

There was a man called Chan-So-Lin
Who lived in a house in China
His little daughter lived with him
And three grown sons beside her.

The daughter was a pretty girl,
Her feet were small and slight,
And on each foot a sandal
Made of silk so thin and light.

Each step she took was fast and airy,
Delicate her poses,
She liked to dance and twirl
In a garden full of roses.

She was a "brilliant flower,"
Said her father Chan-So-Lin,
While her older brothers liked to call her
"Little girl of spring."

When Chan-So-Lin went travelling,
He told his sons: "Protect my daughter,
You three boys, I shall return,
As soon as the Sabbath is over."

Zvi and Naomi Neeman with their daughter Yael.

On the way back to Narcissus, my brothers would plant me in the holes that Eli had dug for the lumquat or pomegranate trees he was going to plant. We played Joseph the Little Brother, who was left in a pit by his brothers. They also taught me the multiplication table when I was three, and trained me to play catch with Gila and Pishta's expensive, unique jars. When our parents went out even for a few minutes, we immediately began a tense game of catch, tossing the breakable jars, four at a time, through the air above the floor. Only the training session took place over the carpet. The game itself (called simply "jars") took place above the floor, and the order in which we threw and caught wasn't permanent, but was decided upon right before we began our daily game.

When we were on our annual, biological family vacation in the kibbutz apartment on Sheinkin Street in Tel Aviv, my brothers used to babysit me one evening per vacation so our parents could go to a concert or a play. "No problem, we'll take care of Yuli," Ofer told our parents. Before that, my brothers and our parents went through all the children's movies that were playing and chose one. But after my parents left, we changed the plan. We never went to children's movies; my brothers looked for the scariest movies and trained me not to be afraid, or we went to see the musical comedy, "Aliza Mizrahi." We liked staying alone, without our parents. We didn't know what you do with grown-ups.

When we had contagious children's diseases—all routines were broken. We'd rest from all the Narcissus activities. We didn't go to classes, didn't clean our rooms, didn't make mush from bread and cold water for the swans and geese in the children's farm. And at 5:30, we didn't go in groups to our parents' houses or see our biological siblings. We forgot that they existed. The outside world sank into itself. And everything was Narcissus, from morning to night.

We didn't go out at all. Our parents would come to us in the children's house. We, all the Narcissus children, were sick together: When we had the mumps, we were sixteen children swollen like pigs; when we had the German measles or roseola, we all had red spots; when we had chicken pox, we all washed ourselves with bowls of gentian violet.

When we had a childhood disease, we tried not to bother Dr. Tzuriel, the kibbutz doctor who worked with my mother, the kibbutz nurse. He was kept for the truly difficult moments, when things got out of control. Not that any of us wanted Dr. Tzuriel to come. My mother said he was very smart and funny, but he scared us. An angry Irishman who always ordered us to undress, and we were cold, so cold.

At 5:30 in the afternoon, instead of going to our parents, they came to us, and the ugly yellow oil-paint walls of Narcissus turned into golden dividers. Our parents were different when they came, maybe because now they were guests in our place, and maybe because they were concerned about our fever, which didn't go down. Those were the only times that my mother read me stories in Hebrew, although she was ashamed about the way she spoke it.

When we had chicken pox, my father told me that when they had them in Vienna, their parents burned their books because they thought that books had something to do with spreading the disease. They burned his copy of *Max and Moritz*. The stories our father told us were filled with life, as if they were three-dimensional, like small shows. And many times, when they were over, they remained present in our rooms, frightening us, as if the happy endings hadn't dispersed them. My father loved to make himself laugh with his stories. He'd get into our beds in the children's house and hide under the blanket and the heavy yellow bedspread. When we sat down on it, there he was. We jumped in fright. In the evenings, after he finished telling a story to all the children in the room and said goodnight, and after the *metapelet* had also said goodnight and gone, he'd stand outside, under the window of our room, and make the sounds of the wild animals he'd told us about earlier, or of the fierce winds that had blown away an entire city and its population in the tale he'd just recounted. We were terrified. We couldn't sleep. Our nights were fear-filled anyway, full of the concerns you should put out of your mind before you go to sleep: We were afraid that terrorists would break into Narcissus, that the Nazis would break into our parents' houses; we were afraid of jackals; we were afraid that the Alon children would come and cover us with toothpaste; we were afraid of Nachman Farkash, the criminal who kept breaking out of prison and roamed the mountains.

Every Purim festival had a unifying "theme" that dictated what the costumes would be and inspired the plays that were written for the holiday. In the third grade, the theme was "peoples of the world." Five of us were Swiss. Our parents came to perform in Narcissus, wearing costumes that coordinated with ours. They were dressed as a delegation of Swiss mountain climbers. Using heavy ropes, they climbed onto our Formica tables, which our imaginations had transformed into glaciers. The yellow oil-paint walls looked like snow-capped mountains. Our parents yodeled a few times, and then my father was lost in an avalanche. The climbers called to him over and over again, but couldn't find him. He was declared "missing." Even though I cried with horror at the loss of my father in a snow avalanche, he didn't appear or peek out for even a moment to show himself. He didn't come back until the end of the evening, clumps of cotton in his hair to represent snow, having miraculously rescued himself from the top of the mountain, so he said, even under the ferocious weather conditions. It wasn't until two hours after Indians skinned tigers in front of us, and Dutchmen stuck their fingers in huge dikes, that my father came in from the cold.

The roseola attacked on Monday, the best day of the week, magazine day. Every Monday, *Mishmar L'Yeledim*, the children's supplement of the *Al Hamishmar* daily newspaper, arrived. When I was sick, my father and I sat together and were carried away into *Mishmar L'Yeledim*.

Since I had a high fever, I told him that I wanted to write a letter to Dvora Omer, the writer of children's books, but was afraid to ask the Questions and Answers column for her address because they always printed the questions and I was embarrassed. So we wrote a letter to the newspaper, asking them to mail Dvora Omer's address to me privately, at the Upper Galilee Mobile Post, and not to print it in the paper. If possible. If not, I thanked them in advance and asked them not to respond at all. To my great surprise, they sent it to me privately.

I wrote a long letter to Dvora Omer in which I told her that I wanted to be a writer. She answered me in her own handwriting (my father stressed that when I complained about the contents). He also pointed out that she'd replied relatively quickly (I think it took about a month, which seemed like an eternity to me), considering that she received many letters from many children. And I pictured my letter drowning in a pile of letters sent by children from all the kibbutzim.

My father said that she'd written me a long letter responding to everything I'd written in mine. All of that was true, but I was very disappointed. Dvora Omer did in fact respond nicely and politely to many of the things I'd written to her, also about the kibbutz. After all, I knew she was from a kibbutz, too. But her response to my statement that I wanted to be a writer pierced me like an arrow. She wrote that you never know where life will lead you. She wrote that she herself had wanted to be a baby's nurse, and she was a writer. So you can never know (she repeated). I considered that letter a deathblow. What does that mean, you can never know? What does that mean, where life leads you? I was very upset by the possibility that I'd be a baby-minder. My father argued that that wasn't what she said, and he was right, but it was no consolation. Logic might help you understand, but it offers no solace.

My mother, who was the kibbutz nurse, told all the Narcissus children: "If your fever doesn't go down by tomorrow, Dr. Tzuriel will come to examine you." Our temperature went down that night, we were all healthy. We didn't want Dr. Tzuriel to come. We preferred him to stay in the clinic or in his house.

10

On our planet, there was no money or talk about money. Money wasn't used as a means of exchange, and there were no salaries.

This is what all the pretty girls from the Oak group sang at Kibbutz Yehiam's twenty-fifth anniversary celebration, glittering in the ultraviolet light, one of the Kibbutz Artzi's innovations in the '60s:

> No, we know nothing about taxes and fees
> But we know about flowers and trees
> We know their value and their might
> Because we were born to the sun
> We were born to the light.

And we, the Narcissus group, sat in the audience, in long rows below the fortress, and watched the Oak girls, mesmerized. At night, when the celebration was over, we went back to Narcissus, and after the *metapelet* said goodnight and left, we got up to rehearse. We sang the song over and over, turned off the light in the corridor, and alternately, in the bedrooms, used the white sheets we removed from the beds in an attempt to achieve even a tiny bit of the divine aura that had encircled the pretty Oak girls. They were three years older than we were, but an immeasurable distance from us. Later, in our beds, we continued to dream about the magical staging of the song, the hand-waving, the turns, the purple light illuminating everything.

In the morning, our dreams about the song were interrupted by the always sudden opening of the shutters by the *metapelet*, and her sharp "good morning," full of yellow sunlight. Some *metaplot* said, "Good morning, time to get up," and others updated us: "Good morning children, three soldiers were killed at the Canal last night. Let's go, get up."

We all got up in unison, sixteen children, eight boys and eight girls; we brushed our teeth in unison, and standing in a silent, well-practiced line, took turns at the sinks, the toilets, in front of the mirror, where the *metapelet* braided our hair impatiently. We waited for Rivka to come to teach us.

Rivka was our teacher from the beginning of the second grade until the end of the sixth. In the seventh grade, we were sent away to the educational institution. We were sent away not only from Yehiam's lovely countryside, but also from our teacher Rivka, and from our golden schooldays, the days of the "Subjects."

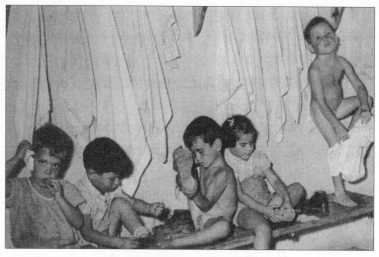

Boys and girls taking a shower together.
Yael's older brother, Ofer, is in the middle.

Rivka loved us all, and never discriminated against or favored anyone. She didn't lose patience or raise her voice. Every Tuesday, we packed sandwiches and halvah and went out for a day-long excursion: to Yanuh through the *wadi*, to Tree Hill, to the duck lake near the fortress, to Anemone Hill, to the bridge, to the bear dens.

We had no exams or grades. The method used to teach us was called "Subjects." Rivka—who also taught the Rock group, Yehiam's first group, as well as the Pomegranate children, who were six years older than us and included my brother Yochai—would switch subjects every month or two, in synchronization and coordination with the other Hashomer Hatzair kibbutzim and the Educational Center in Oranim. Within each subject, we covered other areas of study such as geography and history.

In "World Explorers," we learned about Magellan and Columbus, about the North and South Poles and the equator. We learned that in Australia, the water spins around in the sink counter clockwise. We all chose the country or the explorer we were most interested in, and wrote a paper about him and the country he discovered.

When the subject was "Kadya Molodovsky," we read her poems, which were our favorites, about poor children in the small towns around Warsaw, and we performed them at the end-of-subject party.

During solar and lunar eclipses, we went outside with pieces of glass and sooty mirror fragments to look at the changing shapes of the heavenly bodies. At night, Yoash taught us to pick out the North Star, the Milky Way and Ursa Major.

We observed tadpoles and salamanders in their natural habitats, in the reservoir, or in different-size aquariums and at varying temperatures.

When the subject was "Field and Garden," we prepared the ground for a vegetable garden and planted beds of cabbages, kohlrabi,

The Narcissus group listening to a lecture.

radishes, peppers and tomatoes, and put scarecrows between them to keep the birds away.

When "Fire" was the subject, we split into groups and went out at night to the hills inside and around the kibbutz—including the fortress and Ein Yaakov—and sent signals to each other with flaming torches made from canvas sacks doused with kerosene.

For "We Cook," we learned about the peoples of the world, their cultures and their lifestyles through their food. At the end-of-subject party, we cooked the food of various peoples and invited all the kibbutz members to a restaurant where we served it. They chose their food from the menus we made, and we were their waiters and cooks.

When the subject was "Weather," we learned about cumulus clouds and rain clouds, about winds and dew, and the first and last rains of the season. We went to the orchards to see the rain gauge that Yair Argaman had devised and improved, and we anxiously followed the changing rainfall averages on the precise charts he drew, which appeared in the kibbutz newsletter and on the bulletin board.

When the subject was "Mail," we learned what a stamp, an envelope and a telegram were. We corresponded with children our age, after we picked their addresses out of a hat that was placed on Rivka's desk. At the same time, children in Hashomer Hatzair kibbutzim near and far picked our addresses out of a hat. We all learned the same things at the same time. Our activities and our memories are identical.

I wrote to Rina on Kibbutz Shomrat (three years later, we were both in the Educational Institution on flat Kibbutz Evron, but when we corresponded, we still didn't know each other):

Dear Rina,

How are you? These are the animals we have on our kibbutz:
sheep, a goat, a monkey, rabbits, guinea pigs, hamsters, and
the birds we have are peacocks, ducks, all kinds of geese,
guinea hens, all kinds of chickens, pheasants, pigeons, all
kinds of parrots. If I write down all the names of all the
animals that we have on our kibbutz (the different kinds of
pigeons, for example) the list would be very long.

What kind of animals do you have there?

Your friend,

Yael

We put our letters in envelopes, wrote the addresses and pasted
stamps on them, then watched Rivka Ofir, the technical secretary,
stamp them. We accompanied the envelopes to the red car that
would take them to places throughout the country via the mobile
post, and we waited expectantly for the replies that would tell us
about the animals on the other children's kibbutzim or about the
average rainfall in the big wide world.

The last thing we did on the subject of "Mail" was open a post
office branch and sell envelopes and stationery to the kibbutz members, for paper money. They also bought telegrams, and our messen-
gers rushed off to deliver them to their destinations.

For the subject "We Are Indians," we set up a totem pole camp below
the fortress, split into teams and slept in the tents we put up. We
wore canvas sacks, our faces were marked with camouflage stripes
day and night, our hair was braided and ribbons were tied around
our forehead. We made a peace pipe. We lit a campfire every evening

The Narcissus group playing "We Are Indians."
Yael stands second from the left, in pigtails.

and ate potatoes that we roasted in it. At night, we guarded our Indian camp, two guards for every two-hour shift. The two camp guards on duty were on constant alert: one kept his ear to the ground to listen for noises, the other kept his bow drawn. The guards warned us when enemies were approaching: Nazis, terrorists, jackals or kids from the Oak group, who were always plotting to paint us with shoe polish. We all went out to fight the enemy with bows and arrows. We felt invincible; we were Indians.

When we were learning math or history in class and couldn't listen or concentrate, Rivka would send us outside. "If you feel as if you're disturbing the group," she'd say, "please go outside." At first, we didn't move, either out of politeness or shame. "Outside, please," she'd say in a sharper tone to whoever was disrupting the class. We went out. When the lesson was over, she asked what we'd done outside. We told her that we sailed on a raft in the reservoir, or, if there had been enough of us outside, also from the Terebinth or Oak groups, we played paper chase. She wanted to know all the details, as if she were the one who'd missed the break and the games, and we weren't the ones who'd missed the lesson.

We studied the subject "Bird and Nest" in the fourth grade. They split us into pairs, and each pair observed a nest and, using stenciled pages prepared for us in advance, reported on what was happening in it. Idit and I managed to be together again. They said we were a bad influence on each other. That this would be the last time we'd be together if we didn't learn to stop dragging each other into mischief.

We found a nest near the members' clubhouse, our favorite place. The members' clubhouse was a stone building different from all the other buildings on the kibbutz. It had hidden gardens and steps on both sides, so it wasn't clear what was the front and what was the back. You could picture a servants' entrance and an entrance for the ladies and gentlemen, and a place where cookies were served on the small lawn next to the library. And on the front lawn—or was it the back lawn?—was a white statue of a naked woman.

On that lawn, in a tree next to the statue, Idit and I found our nest. A sparrows' nest. A real nest with fledglings in it.

After breakfast, each pair of birdwatchers (when "Bird and Nest" was our subject, we were all called birdwatchers) was given two hours to watch the birds and write a report that they'd read aloud in class the next day. Those free hours were a temptation for Idit and me, who dragged each other into mischief.

At first we thought, we don't have to spend two whole hours at the nest every day in order to report on what's happening inside it.

And then we thought, actually, an hour is too much. And on the fourth or fifth day, we'd already stopped watching the birds.

We wrote our report every day, part of it entirely fictional. In our nest, the mother brought food for her chicks. The food suddenly dropped out of her beak, and the father would dive down to save it. Falcons (which were plentiful in the fortress) swooped over the nest and endangered the lives of the chicks. Suddenly, after we'd been watching for three days, the father stopped coming. Did he die, we asked the Narcissus children, and also Rivka, who had been listening raptly to our descriptions.

We used the time we were supposed to be bird watching to plan the great break-in—the break-in to the clubhouse. There was only one very obvious reason that we broke into places and committed crimes: candy. We weren't envious of city kids because of their clothes, bicycles or skates. But we fantasized endlessly about candy, the way young boys fantasize about girls, the way young girls fantasize about love. They might not have suspected us, Idit and me, of that break-in, even though we were always dragging each other into mischief, because we were both so skinny. And girls, of course. And also, our reports on the birds and the nest were so believable.

The members' clubhouse was an entire quarry of candy. There, in the closet, was where the refreshments were kept for the members who played chess there, or read newspapers or did other things about which we had absolutely no idea. They would go there after they had supper in the dining hall of their parallel universe. The dining hall and the clubhouse were part of the after-work lives of the members, where they talked about work schedules and holidays, where they mourned, where the endless rounds of anger, accusations, reconciliation and silences took place.

There were huge boxes of wafers and cookies in the clubhouse, and we could simply lift off a layer or two without anyone noticing, or so we thought. But in reality, the break-in was a lot more complicated. The clubhouse was locked, and we had to go in through the window. But the window was visible to anyone who came out the back door of the dining room. Anyone just happening to pass by would catch us.

Climbing up to the window, which was higher than we thought it would be, took a long time because neither one of us could boost the other up to it, and hanging there on the window, we couldn't help each other open the screen, and when we finally got inside, covered in scratches from the rough wall, we had nothing to put our loot in, and we were terrified that we'd be caught.

We just wanted to get out of there, and in the end, we decided to take a full tin of wafers. We didn't break in again, not after we had so much trouble closing the screen when we were outside. For the entire time we studied "Bird and Nest," we lived on a stash of wafers that we buried under the tree where the bird, the fledglings and the nest were perched.

Later, in different contexts, they threatened to separate us again, or send us to a psychologist who, unlike the dentists, didn't live in Nahariya or the northern suburbs of Haifa. They were further away and more expensive. And only when there was no other choice were we sent to them, to Haifa, usually to the upscale Merkaz Hacarmel neighborhood. We were sent to them in the hope of sweeping our problems out of the kibbutz, or at least, to keep the psychologists away from it. The Hungarians didn't believe in psychology or psychologists, who they thought were more like astrologists than healers. Psychology served as permanent comic relief in Zambo's parodies. For example, in the parody he wrote about the famous notebook diary, in which the nursery *metapelet* and the night guards, who were on weekly rotation, exchange instructions and reports on the condition of the babies and children sleeping in the children's houses.

The *metapelet* writes to the guard:

Dear Guard,
Zohara is sick. She'll most likely cry at night (the bed opposite the door). Give her a suppository. Don't forget that she's just a baby and the theory of how to treat babies we once learned in the agricultural college applies only to calves [...]
All the best,
The nursery *metapelet*

And the guard replies to the nursery *metapelet*:

Dear nursery *metapelet*,
You left your book, *Infant Psychology*, in the nursery. I browsed through it, it's very interesting, especially the chapter on bed-wetting during the oral stage. Ronit and Amit must have gone through a very difficult oral stage. I asked them if they read the book. No, they didn't read it. But they still wet the bed three times. Just through healthy instinct. As you instructed, I changed their sheets twice, and the third time, they'd already learned how, and did it themselves.

All the best,
The guard

The children who were sent to a psychologist in the fancy Carmel neighborhood of Haifa were first diagnosed on the kibbutz with "special problems." Sometimes the "special problems" diagnosis occurred after they set the granary on fire, or stole and drove a fire truck, or of course, if they killed an inordinate number of animals or killed them in a manner radically different from the accepted method.

Most of our dogs did not live long.

Many dangers lay in wait for them, both from the children and the adults. In the adult world, there was the person who poisoned them, who was also the vet. There was nothing to be done about that, because he was from there, from the land of the frozen Danube. There were many explanations for what he did. They said, among other things, that it was because there, the Nazis set dogs on him or his family.

Sometimes the poison was left for a specific animal, and sometimes it was spread throughout the kibbutz. They said that he had a certain quota. No one knew exactly how many, or whether it was really a matter of a quota. We didn't know if it was a particular dog, or its color, or the fact of its existence that got on the poisoner's nerves.

We, the Narcissus children, had Barak. We didn't remember who found him and how he came to be ours, or even how we chose his name. We called him Barak. He lived only a short time, but his brief life was a happy one.

When he came to us, he was a tiny puppy and he especially loved our four shoe compartments, which were arranged according to the four rooms we slept in. He would burrow inside them until he grew large enough to live in the doghouse we built for him outside. We left him every day for only one hour and fifty minutes, when we went to visit our biological families as invited guests at 5:30 in the afternoon. At 7:20 in the evening, we returned to Barak, petted and hugged him, and he jumped on us and licked us.

Less than a year later, he died the natural death of all our dogs: he was poisoned. Most of the dogs on the kibbutz were poisoned to death. Either targeted or randomly. The poisoner, who was also the vet, really loved animals, and made sure they were given penicillin when they were sick. Everyone knew that we could call him in the middle of the night, anytime, anywhere, to treat an injured animal, and he would do everything to save it.

When Barak died, we buried him in the plot we'd prepared in front of the place we called "The Lovely Corner," a natural, green lean-to very close to where his doghouse had been. We decided that there would be a seven-day mourning period, a shivah, during which we wouldn't eat sweets between 5:30 and 7:20 in our biological parents' houses. We lasted two days, and on the third, we went back to eating wafers, but we never forgot Barak.

The Oak children had the oldest dog. No one understood what was so special about Kushita, a small black dog, that kept her alive for so many years. In Narcissus, we called her "Dragon-Tailed Kushita." We were jealous of the Oak kids for having their Kushita. Even though she was small, tangle-haired and black, she was alive, she survived.

She survived all the poisonings, both targeted and random, but she didn't die of old age either.

There were several versions of Kushita's death, but they all had one thing in common. A tractor driven by one of the children ran back and forth over her, and it was done right in front of the Oak kids.

Some people said that before she was run over, she was thrown off the top of the silo, which was ten stories high. Others said that before she was thrown out of the ten-story-high silo, she was put in a canvas sack with rocks so she'd fall faster, and still others said that she was put into a canvas sack without rocks so she'd fall slower.

Maybe Kushita's surviving presence was too in-your-face for some people, and maybe her death had nothing to do with that. She died a natural death; it was natural for a dog to die that way on Kibbutz Yehiam: in a fall, run over or poisoned.

None of the grown-ups asked who ran her over, or even how Kushita died. Only the children speculated about the various accounts. When things happened, we never saw them happen. We would turn our backs in order not to know or see; or sometimes it was the other way around, we watched with wide-open eyes without knowing, without seeing. Back-turning was our native language: our backs saw like our eyes. Our eyes were as blind as our backs. And if the grown-ups were looking for one of the children, we crowded around him and around ourselves—we didn't remember and didn't know which one of us did what, or what was done to us or to our dogs.

The Oak group buried Kushita on their favorite piece of land and moved on. The sky didn't fall. Maybe some committee dealt with the driver who ran her over.

When all the committees of the socialist method gave up on those children with "special problems," they were removed from the kibbutz, like the jackals, and exiled to "special institutions."

Our dogs were poisoned by the grown-ups, or dropped like rain from the silo by the children. Nevertheless, we were happy with our

Subjects and with our recesses, when we dashed outside to play on the soccer field, Barak and Kushita running behind us, wagging their tails.

11

Sometimes we were so happy that we would freeze in the air for a second, and glide. The gliding happened suddenly, as we moved. We glided every day at 10:30 in the morning, when we ran through the shortcut to the soccer field after we finished working. We glided when we walked on the goal post on one end of the field, hovering as we balanced ourselves above the ground.

Sometimes we ran to the long, high laundry lines, checking to see that there were no grown-ups around to catch us red-handed as we hung like clothes, our hands clutching the long, strong ropes, while one of the kids turned the pulley so that we rode along them, breaking away slowly from the concrete, then breaking away from the world, our feet hovering high above the ground, our heads spinning in the air.

We glided when we drove in the race cars Zohar and Amram built in the fifth grade: a board on four wheels was the frame of the car, an iron chain served as the steering wheel, and a pole with a rubber-tipped bottom was the brakes. For endless days, we rode on carts from our biological parents' houses back to the children's houses. We said to them: "You don't have to take us back, we have our car here," and we took off, dragging the carts up the hills and flying down them on it, floating over the sharp turns, navigating with the chain, slowing down with the rubber brake.

We started working in the second grade. We worked in our rooms, we helped the *metapelet*, we worked on the children's farm, and in our classroom. We worked on a weekly rotation, in teams of two to four children. Every week, we'd move on to the next job, and so on. The class work consisted of erasing the blackboard, picking up the chairs and putting them on the desks, and washing the floor of the classroom, which was in the Narcissus building, adjacent to our dining room. Helping the *metapelet* was easy work, but had to be done at inconvenient hours. Split shifts. We had to clear and clean the tables after breakfast and lunch in our dining room, then we had to make all kinds of deliveries with the *metapelet*'s cart, bring the sacks of clean laundry from the *communa*, bring food from the dining hall. Each task at a different time.

We hated working in our rooms the most. Our four rooms, each inhabited by four children, one in each corner, were always neat and orderly. We each made our beds and covered them with the thick yellow bedspreads right after we got up in the morning. But straightening things out was only the beginning; the order was meant to expose every corner and every baseboard that would then have to be scrubbed.

During the week we were scheduled to clean our rooms, we washed the floors every day at ten in the morning. After that, the *metaplot* washed them again. Every inch of our rooms was exposed. Except for the nightstands next to our beds, there was nothing. The rooms were spotless, almost sterilized, and the walls were painted in yellow oil-based paint so that they would also be washable. We were constantly told that cleanliness alone was not enough; absolute cleanliness was necessary to prevent the infiltration of germs, which might lead to epidemics in the children's houses.

Children's work included harvesting vegetables.

Our system, particularly the communal sleeping in the children's houses, bred many disagreements, and maybe that was why everyone was so fixated on the cleaning rituals, which focused mainly on the bedrooms, as if the cleanliness proved the success of the children's houses. The cleanliness was much taller and broader than we were. It was the cleanliness of a hospital, of a prison. The head *metaplot*, the temporary *metaplot*, the rotating *metaplot* and we, the children, all functioned as workers in the cleanliness machine.

We swept the floor, then we scrubbed it with a stiff-bristled straw broom, soap and a river of hot water, and then we swept the river out through the corridor.

During the floor-washing ritual, which was repeated daily, we changed the hot water in the pail three times so that it wouldn't be contaminated by the washrags, or the opposite, so that the washrags wouldn't be contaminated by the water. We washed the rag over and over again, wrung it out as hard as we could, and dried the floor with it.

Three of the bedrooms lined the corridor, at the end of which was "the last room"—the one whose door opened onto the length of the corridor—and opposite it at the other end of the corridor was the *metapelet*'s room (where our clothes compartments were, divided according to rooms). From that room, the *metapelet* could, with one quick look, observe everything that was going on in the corridor. Sometimes, when the rotating *metaplot* worked with us, we tricked them with the last room, the fourth one. We used the entrance to the room as a façade: we placed the pail at the door with the washrag on it, as if we were in the middle of washing and would be back in just a second. We spread a bit of cleaning liquid on the floor, and then jumped out the window. From a quick *metapelet* glance from the end of the corridor, everything looked fine, and she was going to wash the floors after us anyway. She could yell at us later, we told ourselves, but now it was time to run. We jumped out the window and ran far away from there, gliding to the field so we'd have as much time as possible to play.

The children's farm, meaning the children's kibbutz (in parallel to the grown-ups' farm, meaning the kibbutz) wasn't a petting zoo as it sometimes seemed to the city people who came to visit us. The children's farm was a kind of exemplar, a smaller model of the farm problems on the kibbutz. There, we were supposed to not only become attached to the animals, but also, and primarily, we were supposed to become educated in work, organization, cleanliness, self-discipline and teamwork, and it was also meant to hone our sense of responsibility (which, in any case, had been honed into the conscience we felt so constantly alive and burning inside us that it became an inner hump).

The plan of those who devised the children's farms also included the setting up of committees, through which the children would receive training in the work of a branch coordinator, work scheduler, treasurer, etc. As usual in our system, the plans were great and visionary, and the shortness of time was their enemy. Nevertheless, we grew attached to animals and loved the work, despite the cold and the smelly mush we made from bread and water and put in tin bowls for the animals.

The animals on the children's farm were chosen on the basis of budgetary considerations, according to the preferences of whoever was in charge of the children's farm at the time, and with an eye to changing fashion. Usually, there were rabbits, guinea pigs, hamsters, peacocks, ducks, various geese, guinea hens, chickens, pheasants, pigeons, sheep, goats, and sometimes, ibexes, miniature deer, parrots and monkeys.

Twice in the history of Yehiam's children's farm, which was founded the same year we were born, in 1960, the animals bypassed the committees and entrance procedures, and came out of nowhere. As if they had been drawn to the children's farm and wanted to join. The first time was at the very beginning. When the Rock children, the kibbutz's first group, went out to work on the children's farm, they couldn't believe their eyes. An exhausted white camel was sleeping at the gate of the farm. The farm was very small then, consisting of only a few rabbits and guinea pigs, and a pair of long-necked geese they called Chava and Yochanan, the names of the two tall kibbutz members of German origin. And suddenly—a white camel. The Rock children gave it food and water, took care of it and loved it from the very first day. A week later, an Arab from Jish arrived and the camel actually ran to him and they hugged each other. The Arab from Jish told them that his white camel had disappeared two weeks earlier. He left fifty lirot for the children in a gesture of thanks for having loved and taken such good care of the white camel that had gone running back to him. The Rock children bought a lamb with the money.

Ten years later, there was a storm with strong winds, and a Barbary duck landed behind one of the kibbutz buildings. The member in charge of the farm said that it must have come from Ein Yaakov (the *moshav* located two kilometers from us, right next to Kibbutz Gaaton, but we'd never been there). At night, we told each other that the duck hadn't come from Ein Yaakov, but from Kansas, like

Dorothy in *The Wizard of Oz*, who flew through the air, together with her house, in a cyclone.

Those were two isolated incidents. Most of the time, our animals, exactly like us, lived exclusively in the Hashomer Hatzair kibbutzim. The people in charge of the children's farms in all the Hashomer Hatzair kibbutzim met for day-long seminars, where they discussed raising animals and the educational aspect of including children in farm work. Those seminars also had a practical side: The people in charge of the children's farms closed deals to trade animals from one farm to another. For example, in one case, Yehiam's children's farm gave Kibbutz Gan Shmuel's children's farm some of our excess ducks and the pheasants that had accumulated, in exchange for a donkey and a male peacock.

We finished our daily work quota at 10:30, and dashed off from the children's farm, from class, and from the hated bedroom clean-up, heading for the large soccer field, to join the Oak, Terebinth and Anemone kids. We ran so we could get in as much playing as possible until 11:15, when the next lesson began.

Every day, we split up into groups and prayed for victory, said magic words and swore oaths, if only we would win.

We didn't know what made us switch games, how and when we decided to move from the dodge-ball season to the tag season to the hide-and-seek season, to the capture-the-flag season, and then to start all over again. We'd grab hold of the games and play them to their depth and breadth, leaping from the ground to the sky, catching the ball, passing the ball, flying in the air, running the bases, hiding behind cypress trees, forgetting everything around us.

On Wednesday, between one and three, there was what we called "a rest from resting," which meant a nap-less afternoon. Once a week, we were allowed to skip the afternoon nap, which we hated so much, and keep playing. All the children in the Children's Society—the Oak, Terebinth, Narcissus and Anemone groups—participated in the games.

But the rest of the time, six days a week, we had to sleep between one and three in the afternoon, or at least be completely silent in our beds. We couldn't read or move or bother the *metaplot* who, during those two hours, folded laundry and put the clothes into our compartments, polished shoes, and did a lot of other things, depending on how quickly they worked and how much we bothered them. We hated those hours of being frozen in place. Time didn't move, or it went backwards on the clocks we didn't have in the children's houses. We kept guessing the time to ourselves, trying to figure out where the minute and hour hands were.

Time also froze at lunch when we were stuck at our tables for a long time after the meal was over because we couldn't get any food down. We felt as if we were stepping on the brakes instead of running, we felt imprisoned. Sitting around the dining room table, we developed a system: We came to our meals with pockets full of small pieces of paper that aroused no suspicion, and we'd slowly pick apart the meat, slip the pieces into the bits of paper, shove the paper deep into our pockets, and in the end, when the *metapelet* couldn't see, we tossed the bits of paper quickly into the trash.

We weren't really scared of the *metaplot* who forced us to eat, we weren't really hurt by the fingernails that dug into our arms when they finally lost patience, or by the way they shook us: One *metapelet* grabbed our hands, the other our feet—and they shook us. So we'd learn to finish our food next time. We thought about other things during the shaking and we swore to ourselves that we wouldn't learn any lessons for the next time.

The *metaplot* were imprisoned in the system together with us, partly prisoners, partly guards. Ever since the early days of the communes, even before the kibbutzim, the women members always found themselves assigned, and assigned themselves, to work in the kitchen, the laundry and the children's houses. To streamline the work on the entire kibbutz and not to disrupt the men from doing their productive work in the fields.

The communes, and later, the kibbutzim, decided that children belonged to their parents, but the responsibility of caring for and educating them fell on the entire kibbutz, and all the women, married or single, participated in taking care of the babies, each in her turn, leaving the mothers free to continue their work on the kibbutz.

Our system was not good to women. On the contrary. The single women, the young women, and even the seventh-grade girls worked in the children's houses, which were always short-handed. The children's houses were supposed to free the woman from childcare, but in fact, they imprisoned them in that work—except that they did it with other women's children. There was equality in women's work, but it existed only among them, the mothers and the single women, and did not apply to the men, except for their Saturday shifts in the children's houses once every five weeks.

During the compulsory afternoon naps between one and three o'clock, we lost patience. We saw the *metaplot* only as guards, and felt sorry for ourselves in our beds. We couldn't sleep, we tried counting the seconds, but they trickled between our fingers. Time did not pass. During those two hours, we hated everything.

Sometimes we got up abruptly, as if our minds were rebelling against our bodies, and our bodies trailed behind them in fear. We couldn't stand it anymore. Sometimes the *metaplot* surprised us by not getting really angry, and they used us to help them distribute clean clothes to their compartments; other times, we were punished and banished to the shower room, to sit there on the bench until three. "It's better than lying in bed," we told ourselves. "At least we tried."

When three o'clock came and the *metapelet* went from room to room, we jumped out of bed totally awake, and skipped outside. We played until 5:30. We played tag, basketball, dodge ball, hide-and-seek, the freeze game, and paper chase, depending on which game was in season and what season of the year it was. In the summer, we played tag in the pool, and the rest of the year, we played it on the lawns.

At 5:30, we went to our biological parents' house, but we didn't stop playing. We ran to the large lawn in front of the row of four small houses where our parents lived, we, the children from that row. Our older brothers and sisters were at the Educational Institution or in the army, and we didn't want to stay in the house, suffocating on the Kibbutz Shomrat Hazorea couches across from the veneer sideboards; we wanted to run. After we wolfed down cake, Anat called me or I called her, and we ran out, every day without exception, to play games we made up. We ran to find things to take to the camp we set up for ourselves on the lawn, a camp for girl soldiers, like the ones who passed through the kibbutz. And once, on one of our search expeditions for equipment for our camp, we passed the Parents' house, which was right next to our biological parents' house.

Real grandparents, who might have stepped out of a Grimm's fairy tale, lived in that house. Old people were a rare sight in our eternally young kibbutzim, the Hashomer Hatzair kibbutzim. Officially, they were called "The Parents," because they were the members' parents, but everyone called them by the only family title that had made its way into the kibbutz, grandpa or grandma. Grandpa Vilmosch, Grandma Guttman.

Some of them were the grandparents of Narcissus children, and the others we saw working on the kibbutz, but we'd never been in their house until that visit. They were few in number, most of them Holocaust refugees who lived on kibbutzim thanks to a humane, bureaucratic Hashomer Hatzair clause that allowed them to live near their families, to fast on Yom Kippur and eat their final meal before the fast in the secular dining hall. We had no synagogues. We were proud that we worked on Yom Kippur and ate wild boar that we roasted on campfires. No circumcision ceremonies were held on our kibbutz. No rabbi set foot on it to perform weddings. The dead were buried in coffins, the Kaddish prayer was not said over them, and any mention of the Bible was forbidden. Secular poems by Natan Alterman, Natan Yonatan or Natan Zach were read at funerals.

Behind the doors to those grandparents' rooms, it was as if the entire setting had been replaced by a strange and different world. They spoke Hungarian almost exclusively. Their cabinets were covered with embroidered Hungarian doilies and porcelain figures. And they had tons of sweets in their cabinets, as if they'd been waiting for hundreds of children to arrive. After that first time, we went to visit them every few weeks. They were always glad to see us, took white porcelain dishes out of their small cabinets and filled them with candies and wafers. On the way there, we picked bits of grass and handed them to them as if they were flowers. We sat for a minute, looked around, ate sweets. Grandma Vilmosch had bleached blond hair, wore red nail polish and pink lipstick, the only woman on the kibbutz who wore makeup. She was allowed, probably because of that humane, bureaucratic clause. She whispered Hungarian terms of endearment to us, and Grandpa Vilmosch laughed. We said *köszönöm szépen* (thank you very much) and ran out of there. No one knew about our visits to that old world, that ancient world twenty meters from our biological parents' houses.

Yael visits the room of a grandparent.

At night, after work and lessons and games, and after we returned from our biological parents' houses and ate supper around the small Formica tables in the Narcissus dining room, and after our biological parents came for the fifteen minutes allowed them and showed us their stopwatches and talked among themselves about work, we went to bed. The *metapelet* sat in the corridor, and all we heard was her voice as she read to us from *Jim and the Train Driver*, or from *The Water Babies*, then said goodnight and left.

We said goodnight, waited a minute for her to walk far enough away, then returned to our lives. At the time, we were preoccupied with the new technique we'd developed to keep us from sucking our thumbs. The four of us in our room ("ours" for that year—every year they'd re-organize the rooms so there'd be equal opportunity), the last room, hadn't been able to stop sucking our thumbs. In the end, we accidentally happened upon the way to do it: We found the *metaplot's* hand cream in their closet, tried it on our hands, and then, when we put our thumbs in our mouth, we discovered that they had a horrible taste. We spread the cream on our hands every night after the *metapelet* said goodnight and left. It did the trick quickly for all of us, except Zohar. He couldn't stop sucking his thumb even with the help of our new technique.

In a most extraordinary step that we couldn't explain and talked about for years afterwards, Zohar was given candy every night to help him in his efforts to stop sucking his thumb. Colorful round pieces of candy in a small dish placed on a chair near his bed. That was how they used to give us all candy once a year, on our birthday. Zohar's candy dazzled our imagination at night, like rare fireflies. We wanted some. Equality had twisted our hearts, and Zohar was tormented by the fact that only he had candy, so he shared it with all of us. We sat on our beds in the last room of the Narcissus group—Ronen, Hagit, Zohar and I—each of us with the most glittering piece of candy in his mouth, and decided that from that night on, anyone who farted after the *metapelet* left had to admit it to all the other kids in the room and tell a story about one subject only—caca. We voted unanimously in favor of the idea. And so our nights became filled with castles of caca, cities of caca, people of caca who did caca things. Until we got tired of that too and moved on to something else.

12

When we were twelve years old, in the seventh grade, everything changed in a single day. We left mountainous Yehiam, we left Narcissus and our teacher Rivka and moved to the Oshrat Educational Institution, which was adjacent to the flat landscape of Kibbutz Evron. We ate there, went to classes there, slept there. We lived there.

We were driven twice a week to Yehiam to work in the fields and the children's houses. Afterwards we went to visit our parents in their rooms, drank instant coffee and ate cake there, then were driven back to the institution. And we went to Yehiam again once or twice a week just to work and come back.

The row of Narcissus kids who used to trail like a centipede behind Rivka to see the arbutus trees on the way to Tree Hill unraveled, and with that unraveling, other activities disappeared: We no longer played soccer or dodge ball on the field; we didn't sail on rafts in the reservoir pond; we didn't sit in a U-shaped formation in class when Rivka spoke or in groups of four around our little Formica tables when we ate.

The countryside changed too, as if all the scenery had been moved aside, exposing an empty stage behind it: There were no fireflies at the institution, no salamanders, no squills, no carobs, no figs, no Judas trees.

Not only was there no nature at the institution, but there was no scenery either. It didn't overlook anything. It consisted of a collection of functional buildings—a dormitory and classrooms for each group, a building that served as a dining room and a building that housed a library and a reading room—surrounded by unimaginative lawns.

We moved to live with 180 youngsters, ranging from seventh- to twelfth-graders, from four kibbutzim (Evron, Shomrat, Gaaton and Yehiam), with that eternal freedom of choice.

We didn't ride to work on Yehiam and back in our GMC anymore, but in a yellow bus belonging to the Mateh Asher Regional District, together with kids from Kibbutz Gaaton whom we picked up on the way down to Evron or dropped off on the way up to Yehiam. Yehiam was always the furthest away, the highest and the most isolated, and we no longer sang "We'll rejoice in Yehiam" on the way to the kibbutz. The song had been left behind at the edge of the horizon of the past, like our baby teeth.

The last of the adults left every day at three in the afternoon, at the end of the school day, and went back to their kibbutzim. We stayed at the institution day after day for six straight years.

Sitting in front of the dormitories at the Educational Institution.

Educational institutions of this type were not common to all kibbutzim, but existed only in those that belonged to the Hashomer Hatzair movement. In 1931, the first such institution was founded on Mishmar Haemek. Our school, Oshrat, was established in 1961. When we went there, in the early 1970s, there were twenty similar educational institutions in the entire country, all built on the same model and given the names of the regions where they were located: Tabor, Gilboa, Ainot Yarden, Maleh Habsor, Mevuot Hanegev and so on.

The educational institution was built on the model of a Hashomer Hatzair independent camp, adjoining one of the kibbutzim, but separate from it. Both the proximity and the separation of these institutions from the mother-kibbutz were deliberate: to distance and protect the youngsters from the decadence of bourgeois life lying in wait for them with their families, and the older kibbutzim that had already become corrupted; and at the same time, to provide them with the opportunity to learn the values of work, productivity and cooperation through a select staff that would convey the educational doctrine in a direct and non-controlling manner.

Each kibbutz was obligated to assign the job of training the future generation to their most suitable teachers, educators and *metaplot*, who together were the educational staff.

According to the Hashomer Hatzair educational worldview, youth is not merely an intermediate stage between childhood and adulthood, but a significant period in and of itself. The educational institution was supposed to give these young people full autonomy, in a democratic setting, to manage their lives independently in the present, and to provide them with the best training for their future as members of their kibbutzim.

Daily life as run by the youngsters consisted of attending classes during the day, working on their kibbutzim in the afternoon and organizing a full social life at the institution in the evening. (In a social structure similar to that of the adult kibbutz, various democratically elected committees were responsible for planning Friday nights, holidays, dramatized trials, choirs, a newsletter, etc.) In addition to their work and social and cultural life, the youths were Hashomer Hatzair counselors in the educational institution and in the neighboring city branches, and volunteered in the surrounding development towns. They chose extracurricular activities they they were interested in pursuing in greater depth and could be studied outside of the institution as well: music, dance, drama, sports and others.

These institutions were called educational institutions, as opposed to schools. The teachers were called workers and educators, the students were called *chanikhim* (derived from the Hebrew root *chinokh*, which means "education") to stress that studies were not the major focus, but only part of the practical and ideological agenda. There were no matriculation exams or final grades. The motivation to study was supposed to come from within and not be imposed from without. Social life and activities in the youth movement were no less important than studies. And all of that was underpinned by our belief in the sanctity of work—three or four times a week, after classes, we worked in the kibbutz fields or children's houses. The system's ideologues saw the educational institution as the last stage in the education and training of a kibbutz member. The boys and girls who graduated from the educational institution had been born on the kibbutz, had absorbed its values from the very beginning, and had not been damaged by the bourgeois institutions of family and education. They would lead the kibbutzim and the city dwellers, who came from the various city branches of Hashomer Hatzair to fulfill their ideological dreams in the kibbutzim, to a better world.

During his years in the institution, the new child would mature into a new man living on a kibbutz, fully connected to and involved in the life of the country. Or, in the words of Shmuel Golan, one of those who shaped Hashomer Hatzair communal education, describing the graduate of an educational institution:

A man of the kibbutz, a man of the soil, a brave fighter, educated, sensitive, a man of the movement and the party, with a personal moral code and a collective conscience, active in all the above mentioned areas.

Children from four Hashomer Hatzair kibbutzim attended the Oshrat

Educational Institution: not in every kibbutz were children born every year. Our group consisted of children from only Yehiam and Shomrat. On the first day of the seventh grade, the ones from Shomrat were welded to us and we were welded to them. There were children we didn't know from other kibbutzim in a number of groups above our grade level. We were a relatively small group, twenty-six children. We weren't called Narcissus anymore, but Seagull. Boys and girls continued to live together, mixed with children from Shomrat, four in a room, one in each corner.

It was difficult for us to talk about the institution in chronological order. We didn't remember the beginning, the way things happened or the reasons for them. Suddenly we were there with the green suitcases we had each received at the end of sixth grade right before we moved. We used the suitcases to take our dirty clothes to the laundry on Yehiam and return the clean clothes. We washed our underpants and bras ourselves in our showers, or we were supposed to. Because of the democratic autonomy of the Youth Society, we did what we wanted to do and didn't do what we didn't want to do. So that we didn't shower every day and we didn't do our wash every day, and that, of course, is putting it mildly.

Slowly, gradually, we also stopped visiting our parents on the kibbutzim. We went to Yehiam, worked there and came straight back to the institution. It was hard for us to bridge the gap between the two worlds. We didn't know whether it was because we missed our old lives or the opposite, because we didn't. We had left civilization and the grown-ups behind us. We sat in the bleachers above the institution basketball court and read the letters our biological parents occasionally sent us with the teachers who came from Yehiam. They sometimes sent a cake with the letters or asked why we didn't come anymore.

We couldn't explain. Psychology and family seemed very distant to us, even fictional, like fairy tales that began "once upon a time." And that notion never dissolved. It was basic, like a prime number. Life there, on green Yehiam, was as alien to us as a visit to our parents, with the piece of cake they always served us on a glass plate and that we ate with a spoon or a small fork, sitting on an armchair or a couch made in the Kibbutz Shomrat Hazorea furniture factory. In the institution, we crossed over to a different cultural bank, completely forgot what a spoon was, or a glass plate or a couch. Our parents on Yehiam asked us not to crack sunflower seeds in the house, if possible. They asked politely. Didn't demand. They said that in Hungary, sunflower seeds were bird food. It didn't seem refined to them. But we had already gone way past refinement; we were in the heart of untamed culture. As if all our actions were made of sunflower seed shells.

Our institution was so barren and beige. Colorless and plantless. From everywhere on the sidewalks we could see the buildings we lived in; we could see anyone standing at the windows. There were no corners. The kitchen was made of stainless steel, the dishes were plastic. We sat in rows around large tables. The noise was as stifling and present as air, as the lack of air. We ate quickly, and if we didn't have kitchen duty on a particular evening (setting up or serving or cleaning up), we ran out of there after five minutes. Sometimes to the Regional Council building, outside of our boundaries, of the institution boundaries, to see flowers. Sometimes we took nocturnal walks to the beach in Nahariya or to Ahzivland.

We no longer worked in our rooms, didn't wash the floor with rivers of water. Just the opposite. Our rooms were a mess; not a single piece of clothing remained in the closets. There were many seasons when we wore only slippers, not shoes, and ate bread that we toasted on the kerosene heaters in our rooms.

At some point, one of the *metaplot* said, "That's it, you've crossed the line," what we were doing was dangerous, and she poured twenty pails of water onto the floor in my brother Yair's room—he was five years older than me—and left him and his three roommates to clear it out. "Now you have no choice but to clean up the room," she shouted, "and then you'll learn."

My brother and his three roommates went from there to *agro-mechanica*, the metalwork and carpentry workshop, and for twelve straight hours, built a system of bridges they installed over the rivers of water. It bridged their room at the end of the corridor to the classroom itself, rose high above the concrete square between the dormitory building and the classroom building and above the spacious lawn. We all went in the evenings to see the breathtaking structure that was illuminated by colored lights that had been planned and installed by a different crew from the same age group who were at the top of their class in math and physics. When all the water had evaporated a week later, they disassembled the bridges. The wood was used for a bonfire.

"Youth is a privilege that goes hand in hand with obligations," was written in large wooden letters in the institution dining room. We didn't know what the privilege or the obligations were.

Suddenly, we didn't know each other anymore. Things would come at us, catching us unprepared. Boys and girls no longer showered together; from the seventh grade, there were two communal showers in every group, one for boys and one for girls.

The smell of our sweat in those days was pungent and our pubic hair was thick and black. Our bodies were changing so quickly that we didn't recognize them. The boys knew us better, saw us more than we saw ourselves. When we undressed at night and dressed in the morning, we would say to the boys, "Turn around." They would turn around politely, 360 degrees, or turn to the wall, to the system of mirrors hidden under the bed.

A ceramic tile fell suddenly from the ceiling of the girls' shower, exposing everything: the boys took it off and put hinges on it, creating a door through which they could climb above the girls' ceiling, the only ceiling that was made of concrete. They drilled a hole in it and set up a little corner for coffee, and opened and closed the door with the help of two magnets.

A few evenings a week, we were counselors, we sang in a choir, participated in a drama club or went to the beach, and there were also many evenings when we didn't want to do anything. We stayed in our rooms, toasted bread on our heaters. Our moods rose and fell sharply, with no warning. As if they were happening outside of us and we were living inside them, and not vice versa.

A new entity—perhaps emptiness, perhaps anxiety—joined us, got stuck to us the way a callus gets stuck in a sock, as threatening as the bite of a poisonous centipede. We were no longer afraid of jackals and terrorists. We were suddenly afraid that life had no meaning. That's what we were beginning to fear. And that fear seemed to become our fifth roommate, a roommate who slept without a bed. The space it took up was different, but it was definitely there. And nothing connected to Hashomer Hatzair could make us feel better.

The dining room in the Educational Institution.

They sent us to talk to Tamar. She was from the enlightened city group that had joined Kibbutz Shomrat. They had degrees in history, psychology and literary theory from Tel Aviv University, and four of them had come to teach us literature, history and psychology. They were a great deal younger than most of our teachers, who had old-style educations from the capitals of Europe.

They were twenty-something, and liked standing and talking with us on the sidewalk. Sometimes they seemed to want to stay at the institution after three o'clock, to keep on talking, maybe even to help us prepare a cultural evening or write an article for our newsletter, maybe even to sleep over.

Tamar wasn't a teacher, but a kind of educational counselor who had her own room in a building at the far end of the institution that also housed the library and reading room. Her job was to listen and refer the problems, to decide whether we had to be sent to a private city psychologist in the upscale Carmel area of Haifa, or to a kibbutz clinic in Oranim.

We were given an "appointment with Tamar," each one of us separately. We sat with her twenty or thirty minutes, however long we managed to last without speaking. We never said a word to her; we stared at the walls, our eyes caught by the poster hanging there, a picture of Freud. When we focused hard on it, a naked woman suddenly emerged from his beard, a kind of allegory of the sexual unconscious covered by the beard that hid his face, jumping out and flooding our thoughts.

We had a lot of time to analyze for ourselves the allegory of the conscious and subconscious in the poster as we sat there, expected to talk and unable to. Our eyes wandered over anything that was outside of us and outside of Tamar. We grabbed onto every neutral surface unconnected to either one of the sides. Sometimes we felt that we were about to speak, that right now, at this very moment, the words, like ants, were climbing up out of our throat. We knew that she was on our side and that if we spoke, she would understand us, but not a single word emerged.

We didn't know what to say. Our thoughts had no substantive form; they were only pieces of something that had no name and no contours, fragments of the same mute but present partner that lived in our rooms, the same anxiety that climbed up our legs, under the causality that explained everything in Hashomer Hatzair. What is the meaning of life, we wanted to ask and couldn't. Not because it was forbidden—it was permitted—but because we didn't know how to talk and we weren't sure that it was even a question. Our thoughts crumbled, had no topic, no subject and no predicate.

No one spoke a word to Tamar. And then came the stage at which she tried to make us talk. She had all sorts of ideas that she brought from the big city. Once, for example, she said: "Speak to the chair."

That set us back immediately. We even stopped contemplating the idea that we were on the verge of speaking.

"You speak to the chair," we told her, or we snapped at her, or maybe we just thought those things and walked right out of there.

We stayed silent. The cases that, based on the system, were classified as very serious, went on to the next stop, which was called "The Center for Child and Family Therapy" in the Oranim Seminary, or in short, "the Center."

Eyal was sent to the Center because after we got on the yellow Regional Council bus on our way to work on Yehiam, he stayed on the kibbutz with the volunteers and didn't want to go back down to the institution because it was ugly, because everyone was the same age and looked the same. He wanted a different plot and different characters. But that was not a possibility. That was forbidden, like running away from the children's houses to the parents' houses at night.

And there was something else: his teacher suspected that he had an "inclination" towards homosexuality. They said "inclination," if they spoke of it at all, as if only the perspective was slightly skewed and they had to fix the slant and the angle, to readjust and realign what had slipped to the side.

The social worker at the Center tried to defeat the problem: she told Eyal that he could fantasize about men but it was important that his sexual experiences be with women.

Eyal, who danced differently from everyone else—so beautiful and free.

Three years later, when he told us he was gay and that's why he liked to stay on Yehiam with the volunteers, he said that the Center was important to his story. Because it was there, in his conversations with the social worker, that he saw how great the gap between the two of them was, and trying to bridge it, which he couldn't, would mean giving up on love, giving up on himself. He also said, "When I left those sessions where she tried to fix me, I was full of homosexual lust. All the words she spoke so clinically and with alarm disguised as the openness of 'in this room, you can talk about anything,' words and expressions like 'homosexual' and 'fantasies about men,' seemed to float up out of my thoughts and grow into colored soap bubbles and candy. My imagination rose up like a giant wave and I left there torn apart with longing for the future, for things I still hadn't experienced. I went straight from those sessions to Memorial Park in Haifa to try everything among the bushes. I felt how the love I yearned for was getting closer from week to week and I called for it constantly, like saying a prayer, every night when I cried to the music of Leonard Cohen."

Eyal was expelled and sent to another Hashomer Hatzair institution. Further away. From there, so they hoped, it would be more difficult for him to get to Yehiam and the volunteers. And if he didn't get to Yehiam and the volunteers, maybe he would straighten out, they hoped.

Every summer vacation we worked on Yehiam and lived on the edge of the kibbutz, each group in its own building. For two months, we went back to being Terebinth and Narcissus and Anemone. Eyal was part of the Anemone group, a year behind us, and he told us, the Narcissus girls, that he was a homo. He told us while we were arguing about whether or not Leonard Cohen was a homo. We weren't sure if we had realized that Eyal was a homo before he told us, if we had felt it when he danced differently from everyone else, so beautiful and free. We weren't sure that had anything to do with it or not.

We explained things to ourselves. What we explained to each other, we didn't understand. There were always those same misunderstandings that we passed on from one to the other like in the games of broken telephone we used to play in the Children's Society, when we would whisper in the ear of the girl to our right the sentence that had just been whispered to us by the girl on our left, and at the end of the circle—when the sentence was spoken out loud and compared to the one that had been whispered at the beginning of the round—it turned out that it had been distorted into a different version of the original.

Eyal was clear and simple; he told us his sentence, said he was a homo. But we weren't sure that we understood. Not because he was a homo, but because of love. We weren't sure who it was we loved. Whether Netta really loved Micah. She said she didn't know how a person knew.

13

We worked, played musical instruments, performed, danced, wrote for the newsletter, wandered incessantly, but nevertheless, the days in the Institution were endless and unbounded. They began early in the morning, ended late at night, and included almost no schoolwork.

Our studies were wedged inconveniently during the day, didn't flow naturally from within as the system had hoped.

Margalit was our *metapelet*. She came every morning on the Workers Association bus from Kibbutz Shomrat, walked down the exposed concrete sidewalks to our building, Seagull, and into our rooms.

Usually, the *metaplot* didn't wait even a second before coming to wake us in the morning. Just the opposite, they used all the momentum they'd accumulated on the way, and always did it loudly.

But Margalit spoke quietly, almost in a whisper, and her steps were as weightless as a cat's. First she floated down the length of the corridor, peering into our bedrooms, checking that we were alive, that we'd all returned in one piece from our nocturnal wanderings inside and outside the Institution, and only then did she begin to wake us, going from room to room.

Margalit was one of the veteran Hungarians of Kibbutz Shomrat; for her, "life" and "health" came before "getting up quickly for work." She spent six straight years with us, from our first day in the seventh grade until our last day in the twelfth, and knew exactly who got up and who didn't, and for which classes. Because just as there were different learning levels in our classes—Level One, Level Two—there were different depths to the levels: There were those who got up on time for the first class and generally got up early; those who got up sometimes, according to a certain pattern (known only to them and perhaps also to the *metapelet*); those who got up sometimes, arbitrarily; and those who never got up.

Margalit pretended not to remember who got up and who didn't, and every morning, she tried again to wake everyone. She didn't argue with those who didn't get up, and tried to wake them again for their next class.

She had an odd habit: She brought jackets from Shomrat with her, and hung them on the central coat rack in the corridor, as if she'd forgotten them there by accident. She didn't talk to us because she knew we wouldn't talk, but she didn't turn her back on us either, didn't sermonize, didn't leave us for even one day. Except for the six months when she suddenly vanished from our lives. They said she'd come down with a rare skin disease and her entire body was covered with the signs of it. A rash? Pus? Vitiligo? We whispered our speculations to one another because we didn't understand exactly what had happened to her. We never spoke to her about her illness, not even on the day she returned.

She never asked us to give back the jackets she brought us, on the contrary, she always made it clear that they were there if we got cold (we were always cold). She turned on the heaters in the shower rooms every morning before she woke us. "The heaters are on," she'd say every winter morning for six years, "Maybe it'll be a little less cold here."

We stood in line for the bathroom and the two shower rooms, boys and girls, brushed out teeth, thrust our feet into slippers or flip-flops, made ourselves instant coffee, and went to class, five meters from our rooms, dragging our feet on the floor, slouching along behind them. We were the wrong way round: Our shadows always preceded us, and we always meandered along behind them. We could never concentrate on schoolwork.

Tom, who wasn't in our group, wrote on the wall above his bed, in huge letters: "THE OPPOSITE." He made it a rule never to go to class, not to establish a precedent that might add his name to the unwritten list of the kids the *metapelet* still tried to wake up in the morning.

He said that there had to be something else, something that was the opposite, or at least different, that this couldn't possibly be all there was. He also said that as we walked along the peripheral road that encompassed the view-less Educational Institution. And as he said that there had to be something else, that this couldn't possibly be all there was, he lay down in the middle of the path, in the middle of his sentence. He suddenly collapsed, as if the words and thoughts were bullets that had caught up with him.

Eli Sagi admired Tom's "THE OPPOSITE." That was his motto too. He said, "First say the opposite, then make a counter-offer, something affirmative, if possible. If not, you should definitely check the negative. Start with the negative," he advised.

He was our history teacher. A Hungarian, one of the founders of Gaaton, a member of the First of May core group that had been split among several kibbutzim: Yehiam, Gaaton and Yasur. Some of our parents and some members of Gaaton, which were two kilometers apart, knew each other from Hashomer Hatzair in Budapest. As if Buda and Pest had become Yehiam and Gaaton, and the Danube had become the Gaaton River.

Eli Sagi really liked the bridges my brother and his pals built to avoid washing their bedroom floor. He was their homeroom teacher. When they were caught smoking in the Educational Institution and were suspended for a week, he was angry at them. He told them that on the kibbutz, it doesn't matter what a person does, it matters what people think he does. If the sign says "No Smoking In or Around the Institution," you should smoke outside, a meter away from the fence. "As far as I'm concerned," he stressed, "you can smoke a horse's prick, just as long as they don't see you doing it here." He said it was stupid to get caught for something so basic. In class, he always asked us not to be stupid, and he used curses instead of prepositions because when he told us not to be stupid, he was thinking about all the stupid things we did, which made him angry all over again.

Eli Sagi said that Hungarian curses were vulgar, which was a compliment for Hungarian, because curses should have feeling. He threw our textbooks at the wall and cursed. His cursing was like a lament, as if with every string of curses (each curse sprang from the previous one and ignited the one that followed it), he was really destroying or mourning the old bourgeois world that had been destroyed anyway for the Hungarians who came from there. (We didn't know a thing about the former lives of the teachers, not only because we always lived separately from the grown-ups, but also because Eli, like Nehama, our home room teacher, were from a different kibbutz and we never saw them living their everyday lives.)

On Friday nights, we held cultural events in the dining hall. We moved the tables to the side, arranged the chairs and participated enthusiastically in the performances. The Institution's cultural committee chose the theme. (The committee members rotated, the themes remained the same: seasons of the year, holidays, etc.)

Having the theme decided for us was actually an advantage. It always began with our refusal, internal and external. We said to whoever spoke to us, or to ourselves: "This time we won't write," "This time we won't do it," "What a stupid theme." But later, as the deadline approached, we felt uncomfortable about it—after all, everyone had to be on a committee and we rotated, and we felt ill at ease, so we did it, reluctantly at first, just to fulfill the obligation, and then we got caught up in it, in the rehearsals. When the performances were over and the chairs had been piled up and moved to the sides of the dining hall, the dancing began.

Before the dancing, during the performances, Eli always stood mesmerized at the far end of the dining hall and asked us not to block his view. He liked to watch and hear everything. He came so he could give us his critique afterwards.

We, the seventh graders, the Seagull group, appeared for the very first time at an Institution show called "Autumn Evening." Every group wrote its own play and performed it. Ours contained only two words and lasted two seconds. All the members of Seagull lined up in a row, and I stood next to the microphone, a serious expression on my face, as if I were about to speak about autumn or recite a poem. I said "Falling leaves," and all the boys dropped to the floor as if they were falling leaves. We walked off the stage and Eli leaped up, shouting a resounding "Bravo" from the far end of the dining hall. He offered me a trade: I didn't have to go to class—I never listened when I was there anyway—and instead, I could read whatever literature I wanted that dealt with history. (He said, "Literature and history, they're cousins; the French use the same word for both—*histoire*.") We agreed on *War and Peace*. He said that sitting in class could destroy people for the rest of their lives, and a book like that could teach us to think about history the entire time we're reading, even if we just think about the title for a second before we open the book.

Eli taught us the art of bartering. He said, "Don't do what you don't want to do. Offer a counter proposal." And that's how we traded later, in the city. We tried to exchange the things we hated for other things.

After reading books instead of sitting in class, we went with Eli for a walk along the Educational Institution's sidewalks and talked about the books, then received a new list based on what we were interested in.

Usually, we didn't actually abandon our schoolwork, not all at once, not as a declaration, but we dropped out, slipped away, as if our hold on it had loosened when it came to listening in class, or even just going there. Even if we did enter the classroom to listen, to grasp the continuity the teachers were talking about and maintain the appearance of being serious students, we caught ourselves floating. The teachers' sentences would crumble in the air, the thread broke, and we, who were somewhere else, reading books or writing letters, were constantly thinking about unrelated things.

Many of the things happened on the sidewalk. The French teacher stopped me on the sidewalk and said we had to talk. I was afraid of talks in general, and of one-on-one talks in particular. I said, "Oh, I forgot to tell you that I'm not taking French anymore." He said, "Excellent, that's exactly what I wanted to tell you." *Au revoir*.

Instead of grades, we were given evaluations. The physics teacher didn't write an evaluation, but at the end of every year, he drew each of us a picture composed of a rear end and a head, either a small rear end and a large head, or vice versa. The first meant that you didn't sit in class but were very smart, and the second meant the opposite. In the small Level One physics class, the boys gave themselves rhymed pedagogically relevant nicknames: Kfir Ampere, Amnon Cyclotron, Carmel Decibel, Tamir Light-Year.

I didn't solve the end-of-year math problem in the ninth grade, but instead, wrote a few lines to the teacher. He definitely wouldn't be able to understand, I wrote, he couldn't get his head around it, but the fact was that I didn't know a thing. At least right now. Maybe I did once, a week ago, but now I didn't remember anything. When he returned my paper, he'd written that he definitely understood, he remembered what it was like to be sixteen, and better luck next time.

But there was no next time. By then, I couldn't listen or solve problems. Before I left math and physics for good, I tried to park on Level Two for a while. That lasted half a year, and then I spent another year on Level Three, which was really small and pleasant. We had one teacher who called Level One "Galloping Level One," and she called Level Two "Level One," so we wouldn't feel as if we were trailing behind.

Our homeroom teachers and our *metaplot* tried to convince us not to leave our schoolwork, not to give up. Nehama was our homeroom teacher, as well as our English and art history teacher. With her, we learned all the tenses in English and all the types of Doric and Corinthian columns. But we couldn't listen or do homework. During homeroom classes, she talked to us about Erich Fromm and Jorge Semprun, about fleeing from freedom and not fleeing from freedom. We liked our homeroom classes; they were about poetry and literature, as if they had been tailor-made for us, and in addition, we didn't have to remember anything for the next time. That was an advantage, because we forgot everything we learned. We couldn't concentrate.

Nehama was from Gaaton, an Israeli who was a great deal younger than Margalit and Eli, the Hungarians. The staff from the Workers' Association sometimes found it difficult to leave in the afternoon. They were sometimes troubled by things we said and did, by the thought that something might happen to us. There still weren't any telephones on the kibbutzim, only one phone in the secretariat office, and The Educational Institution secretariat office was only open in the morning.

Nehama, Eli, Margalit and the other teachers tried to persuade us not to leave our studies completely, to maintain some kind of connection with every subject, but when they saw how determined we were, they agreed with us and didn't mention it again. They knew that later, after the Institution, our first and last step out of the kibbutz world would be to the army, and then we'd return. The enormous, total freedom that spread now from the sea at Ahziv, to the sky and to Haifa, six whole years, would end abruptly. We would no longer be able to choose what to study and what not to study, because on the kibbutz, you learned a profession that the kibbutz needed; nor would we be able to choose where to work, because on the kibbutz, you worked where workers were needed.

We weren't thinking yet about how life would be. They already knew.

The following item about the Educational Institution appeared in our kibbutz newsletter (and similar items appeared in other kibbutzim newsletters):

> Many kibbutz members claim that our children are edu-
> cated for many years, but when they complete their studies,
> they do not have a profession. That is true, we tell our chil-
> dren—and this is said explicitly to those who wish to learn
> a profession—because that is how they will best serve the
> interests of the kibbutz.
>
> Because the only profession is being a kibbutz member.
> And all of you, when you become members of the kibbutz,
> will be directed to the work that is required of you.

The last of the adults left the Institution at three in the afternoon, on a Regional Council bus that took them eastward, toward the hills, to Gaaton and Yehiam, or slightly southwards, to Shomrat.

In the evenings, we went out, wearing Margalit's jackets, to take in a bit of air, to stretch our legs, to wander. Sometimes, there were concerts and performances in the Kibbutz Evron hall.

Once every two weeks, there was a movie in the Institution. We saw Godard and Bergmann in our dining hall. The tables were moved to the sides again, the chairs arranged in rows, and the dining hall became a movie theater. The screening of Hitchcock's *The Birds* turned into chaos during the climactic scene, when the screen filled with flapping birds' wings. Real birds were released into the dining hall through the windows, and covered us all. The boys in the Dekel group, two years older than us, were responsible for the onslaught. They wanted to see whether Noam's heart (Noam suffered from heart disease and was not allowed to be upset) would withstand the fright. It did.

The boys from Grove, one grade above us, asked the girls in our group to be their girlfriends. In the eighth grade, Tali appeared once every few weeks and whispered to one of us, "Tamir wants to be your boyfriend," or "Gilad wants to be your boyfriend; be at the bus stop at eight tomorrow night."

Students from the Educational Institution on a bicycle excursion.

The bus stop was near the Institution's dining hall. The yellow buses that took us to work on the kibbutzim and back left from there. And it was from that bus stop that we set off on our walk along the peripheral road that encompassed the Institution in the most circular manner possible. In other words, it didn't lead anywhere, but ended up in the same place it started.

We didn't know whether the Grove boys really wanted to be our boyfriends, or whether the idea was all Tali's—she was in the Grove group too. The matches were more sociological than romantic. Who should be with whom, who deserved to be with whom. We, Gilad and I, weren't sure who initiated the proposal; nor were we sure what the proposal was. But we didn't talk about it. We talked about the fact that we didn't actually have a relationship. We met twice and broke up easily, like two subjects participating in the same sociological experiment.

When we returned, we realized that we'd come back to the same place on the circular path, which was really nice—not only had a boyfriend-girlfriend relationship been proposed, but no damage had been done. There we were, we'd taken a walk and returned to the same spot, and nothing had happened. But later—it's difficult to say when—the way we stared at the ceiling was different, empty and thick at the same time. We had a thought followed by a contradictory one, and they spun around rapidly in our minds, like a sled colliding with an obstacle: maybe I don't want him, but he doesn't want me either. Why doesn't he want me? And if I care, does that mean I want him? Maybe, maybe, maybe. We had set off arrogantly on the circular path of love, and we returned heavier, as if years had been added to our lives, as if we had taken part in a non-existent war.

We wanted to stare at the ceiling and think endlessly about what had happened. And the more we stared and thought, the more we stayed in the same place in the loop, still asking the same question: But what actually happened there? As if the answer didn't lie in the plot or the background, but in the folds of something hidden.

The *metaplot* no longer read us stories at night. We read Pinchas Sadeh, Herman Hesse, Dostoyevsky. We wandered. Sometimes we hitchhiked to Haifa and Ahzivland, and once, we rode back from Nahariya in the morning inside one of their touristy horse-drawn carriages, arriving before classes and before Margalit woke us. Our movements were slow, strange, lethargic. We were moonstruck. Our moods swung from hot to cold and back again.

The habit of saying hello to grown-ups who walked by was still ingrained in us.

In the Institution, at night, we said hello to the hired night guard who patrolled the sidewalks. He was the only grown-up there at night. Once, when we met him on the concrete sidewalk, under a huge moon, and said hello, he told us his story, even though we hadn't asked. He said that he had nightmares and couldn't sleep anyway, so he became a night guard. He told us he was from Argentina and asked if we knew what was going on there. We didn't, we were ignoramuses, preoccupied with our own things, our thoughts on our life, work, school, on who loved whom, and we were preoccupied with our moods, which seemed to come out of nowhere, as if the seasons of the year existed in our bodies and kept changing, without the regularity of seasons. We were preoccupied with our fears, which began then, that perhaps nothing had any meaning.

"People get lost there, they're kidnapped right off the streets," the night guard said. "They disappear, as if the earth had swallowed them up. They're probably locked up in cellars and tortured to death." It was obvious that the guard's rifle posed a danger only to him. "That's horrifying," we said, "and there's nothing anybody can do?"

"Nothing," he said, and suddenly began to weep. We didn't know what to say. So we said goodnight. "Goodnight," he said. And we continued our wandering.

14

After supper and the cleaning-up shift, when the large sinks were empty of water and dishes, we occasionally invaded the ugly stainless steel kitchen and made French fries. We called that "the kitchen break-in" because the kitchen in the Educational Institution was locked at night.

We left traces at the crime scene—grease stains—that gave us away, and every now and then the homeroom teachers and the grown-ups caught us. We admitted to making the fries, but we kept the other things to ourselves: They never caught us in Ahzivland, where we sometimes went from our autonomous country in the Oshrat Institution, and they didn't search for us in Nahariya, to which we went on foot, or in Haifa, to which we hitchhiked.

Everyone preferred the story of the kitchen break-in over all the other stories, which had no clear boundaries or motivation. It was sexless and bloodless, free of violence, drugs and alcohol, free of problems and conflicts between man and his fellow man, and was in fact free of good and evil—it was a neutral story.

The next stage was an inquiry. They talked to us about trust and break-ins that violated it and were contrary to openness. We replied whatever we replied. The homeroom teachers' questions and our answers were polite, almost bored.

When the inquiry was over, our parents were asked to come from the kibbutz for a "talk with the principal" of the Educational Institution, in an act composed of patched-together vestiges of urban bourgeois life that had no connection to anything in our world, like single beads without a string, without a plot. Beads that had rolled in from another story. After all, parents never set foot in the Institution, except for several regular, well-planned occasions over the years (to celebrate our graduation, for example).

The punishment was always the same, though they supposedly gave it much thought and consideration each time they imposed it: a week's suspension from the Institution.

During that week, we worked full time on the kibbutz. That punishment, being suspended from the Institution, was considered a sign of heroism, both by us and the kibbutz members, who had to restrain themselves from patting us on the back. Everyone knew, after all, that work was more important than school, more important than anything.

On Yehiam, where we lived when we were on vacation from the Institution, and worked mornings for two-thirds of the vacation, our lodgings were located on the edge of the kibbutz, on the side of the hill closest to the fortress and the pool. We lived three in a room.

Getting up for work was the opposite of getting up for classes. There was no feeling of vacation. We felt obligated long before we got up, before the alarm clock rang. We got up feeling pressured, responsible. The sound of the alarm clock blended into our dreams, became intertwined with them. First we dreamt that the ring of the alarm clock was a siren. Then we dreamt that we'd fallen asleep when we had to get up for work, and then we startled awake and jumped out of bed.

We got up and dressed, our bodies hurting inside because of the early hour, four or six in the morning (depending on the work and the season), then we walked to the dining hall, drank dark tea from plastic cups and sat down in the truck, hoping we'd never get there, though we knew we would, then wishing we were on the way back.

For the boys who worked there regularly, the fields were a world unto themselves, filled with responsibility, competition, pride, humiliation, driving tractors, operating the various machines. Each year, they were assigned to a more complicated, more prestigious agricultural branch. For us, the girls, the work day was clearly defined and permanent: We worked in the children's houses most of the time, and we only went down to the fields in a particular season and according to the changing needs of the various branches. Everything was known in advance. Everything was quantified, like the rows and furrows and how much the harvesters managed to pick, or they were measured, like the pears that we measured, each and every one, to make sure they were large enough to be picked. Measured like the pails and backpacks and the containers we filled and emptied into large crates, then went back to fill again.

Bananas, oranges, pears, avocados. The trees, the fruit. The baskets, the backpacks, the containers, the regular ladders, the power ladders, the knives. We climbed up and down, and emptied the baskets and pails and backpacks into the crates. We worked according to the seasons: Sometimes we irrigated, sometimes we tied, sometimes we packed. We picked, removed stones, pruned. We could barely concentrate; we thought about the upcoming breakfast, then about the ten o'clock break, then about lunch. Time will pass; after all, it always passes. Think only about the fruit, the sack. The regular ladders and the power ladders reached all the way to the sky; the tractors drove through mud, through furrows, on the sidewalks and inside our heads, plowing our thoughts. The air was clear.

As the day wore on, the difficulty became worthwhile; it was tangible, you could touch it, as if it had merged with the prize that followed it, and the sweat of fieldwork had its own unique taste, the deep satisfying taste of the field kitchen breakfast, the sweet taste of reward.

But the most important, most valued reward was the objective, momentarily calming proof of a job well done. That kind of proof was given in a written report on our performance, where quantities were written down in detail and compared to the adults' averages, similar to the newsletter report on the Rock and Grove children, the two first groups on the kibbutz, when they worked in the orange groves for the first time:

During the Hanukkah vacation, the Rock/Grove children went down to pick lemons. They put in 9.6 days of work in only three days, during which they picked 140 field crates—a decent output that does not fall short of an adult's average output.

The competition between the boys and girls was conducted in an orderly and disciplined manner. For us, this is a good sign for the future, when we want to do harvesting work with our children in the Educational Institution [...] We can learn from this brief experiment what we have known for a long time—the great importance of involving our children in agricultural work. And the results are extremely positive, not only in educational terms, but also, and primarily, in farming terms. During those few hours of work, the Rock children proved themselves very able, as they did in other jobs they performed. The orange grove workers will welcome them with open arms any time.

But most of the time, the girls were sent to work in the children's houses.

The children's houses had long corridors, no horizon and no seasons. No one wrote words of praise for the *metaplot* and their achievements in the newsletter. No laundry-folding or shoe-polishing records were ever acknowledged.

From one o'clock until three, we helped the *metaplot* who were in charge of waking the children: We polished rows of children's shoes (a row of brown and row of red), folded the laundry that came in sacks from the *communa* and distributed it to the compartments. Our eyes were on the compartments in the *metapelet*'s room, where we placed the folded laundry, but the fear came from behind our backs, from the direction of the corridor. We were afraid we wouldn't finish the job, that one of the children would wake up and slow us down. We wanted to finish distributing the laundry and do other special cleaning jobs before they woke up in pain, or with problems or unexpected desires we might not know how to fulfill.

In the sixth grade, we ourselves had still been in the children's houses; in the seventh, we were made assistants to the *metaplot*; and in the eighth grade, we were *metaplot*. Women and girls worked in the children's houses, where more helping hands were always needed.

Mistakes you made in the children's houses were unlike mistakes you learned from in other jobs, in the fields, working with tobacco, in the kitchen or the gardens. Mistakes in the children's houses had a ceaseless melody that began before work and continued after it. The threatening melody of a barely averted disaster that might still happen.

Once, one of us put a boy in a bathtub of boiling water by mistake; another time, one of us forgot a child on top of a missile. It was a tall missile that had been built for the kibbutz children's holiday. The children's holiday was an addition to the kibbutz holiday, another celebration of the kibbutz enterprise. The tall missile was the pride of all the children's holidays. It was four stories high, with a spiral staircase that took climbers from one story to the next, which grew progressively smaller. The boy was forgotten on the highest landing, at the top of the missile. He was three.

He was rescued when his screams were heard by a passerby. He'd apparently been there for fifteen minutes. That was our groupmate's first day of work with those children as an assistant to a replacement *metapelet*. They had both taken the children to the playground, to the swings and the missile.

The boy's mother told our groupmate about it at supper. She didn't reprimand or lecture her; she simply told her about it quietly, as if she were telling her a story about another child on a different kibbutz with a different *metapelet's* assistant. She didn't talk about

Working in the kitchen at the Educational Institution.

it with any adults on any committees, not even with the regular *metapelet*, and there was no investigation. We were apparently saved, and nothing happened. We were in the eighth grade then.

We talked about it on the yellow bus that took us back to the Educational Institution. We felt that we should think about all the things that could happen when we were in charge of a large group of children. We thought we should count them constantly; after all, even in our Narcissus group, Izhar had been forgotten once and left on the Ahziv beach. We should have learned then, we told ourselves. But we're only assistants to the *metaplot*, we said, trying to calm each other down, you can't learn everything in a single day. But we didn't calm down. We relived mistakes in our minds, the way we had relived the goals we made or missed in the Children's Society on the soccer field the previous year. We wanted to excel without making mistakes, not small ones and certainly not mistakes like that. There were no records set or broken in the children's house. It was a level plane with no horizon.

The veterans who worked in the fields, the children's houses, the dining hall and the shoemaking workshop, in all the workplaces had accumulated hundreds of days off. We, on the other hand had just begun to work, along with members of the other groups who were becoming part of the system, and volunteers who had been infected by it, and we felt unworthy of it. There was no end to what you could do because initiative could always find more and more ways to be productive. Even if we finished all the obvious things, like folding all the laundry or polishing all the shoes, wrapping all the bunches of bananas and picking all the citrus fruit—there were always more and more special projects, and when they were finished, there was an endless number of more efficient, improved ways to do them.

Just as there was no beginning or end to work, so it was with us. It was difficult to differentiate between us and work.

We were afraid to ask questions about work, afraid to be a burden, to slow down the grown-ups, to diminish their productivity, to stop the system from moving forward.

We never satisfied the system, mute and gentle as it seemed, never asking anything for itself, seeking only to be considerate, to make no demands: "Each according to his ability." But who knows how to truly measure ability; it has no bounds or limits. Our system was never satisfied. We felt guilty.

Work demanded not only diligence or a particular number of skills. We could acquire some, the ones that could be learned, but it was more like an additional sense, an additional dimension, an additional organ. It was both outside and inside us. As if work were above us and encircled us. We were replaceable; it was not.

The Hashomer Hatzair enterprises were identical and functioned in total synchronization. All of us, from all the kibbutzim and educational institutions, moved from place to place in perfect coordination. We did so in our sixth grade hospitality program. We did so on our week-long annual trips and in camp during the summer vacation with the Children's Society: We went to camp in Kibbutz Zikim, swam in their pool, jumped off their diving board and slept in their beds, and they came to Yehiam, played tag in our pool, ate around our Formica tables and slept in our beds. We switched places only with them on our planet, the kibbutzim of the Kibbutz Artzi Hashomer Hatzair movement.

In the seventh grade, when we were twelve and went to the Educational Institution with fourteen other children from Kibbutz Shomrat, and another 160 older kids from Gaaton, Yehiam, Evron and Shomrat—of course, they were also from the Kibbutz Artzi and Hashomer Hatzair—we learned that their childhoods had been filled with the same personal experiences that had filled ours, and later, on the movement's excursions and in the seminars on Givat Haviva, we met many more who shared the dream that was our lives.

The more our world seemed to expand, the narrower it became, until it was like a world of fun-house mirrors. Our private lives were reflected in the dreams of others: our older siblings, people from kibbutzim in the far-off Negev desert, in the Sharon area, in the entire country. Everyone had private memories of the night guard who didn't come or who came at the wrong moment, and everyone pretended to be asleep. We all remembered the same recorder song books and the upside-down day when we stayed awake all night, until dawn, and we all remembered the rest from resting every Wednesday, when we were allowed to skip our nap between one and three in the afternoon and could keep playing on the field.

It was as if the cards were shuffled every time, mixed well, but still—with impossible probability—we were all dealt totally identical cards. That's why the Week of Broadening Horizons seemed so glittering to us. We didn't switch places. We traveled. Not only did we travel, but we went to places that were very different from ours: an Arab village, a religious moshav, a young kibbutz, and Tel Aviv.

Apparently the repeated debates on the status of work as opposed to that of society and culture were what caused the various institutions to add letters to the acronym WBH (Week of Broadening Horizons): WBWH (Week of Broadening Work Horizons); WBSH (Week of Broadening Social Horizons); and WBCH (Week of Broadening Cultural Horizons).

For two or three days in the tenth grade, four days in the eleventh and a week in the twelfth, we learned, worked and lived inside the new shape we were exposed to, we lived a different life.

In the tenth grade, all the members of the Hashomer Hatzair educational institutions traveled (each separately, unaware that the others were doing the same) to a nearby Arab village. We went to Tamra for two days.

Although Tamra was only nineteen kilometers from the Oshrat Educational Institution in Evron, we knew hardly anything about the boys and girls our age who were hosting us. Nor did we know what to ask, where or what to begin with: the end of the 18th century, when, according to the local tradition, the place was founded? Or maybe 1948, when many residents who had been driven away from the surrounding area had joined them? Or 1956, when Tamra was officially designated a local council? Despite the "brotherhood of peoples," such an intrinsic part of kibbutz doctrine, we neither knew nor learned the history of the neighboring Arab villages. They knew a great deal more about us. Our hosts' parents were "one of us"—some of them were paid workers on our kibbutzim, the Hashomer Hatzair kibbutzim.

In the morning, we went with them to their huge school, which was so different from ours: Its walls were exposed and peeling; it was cold because there was no heating; the equipment was broken. We had a literature and a geography lesson with them. In the literature class, we learned Bialik for the first (and last) time in our lives, and in the geography class, we learned about the structure of a port city, we learned that it was logical to build one that backed onto land.

In the evening, we paired up and walked to their houses with them. There was a TV in every house, not like on the kibbutz—one in the entire Institution. That evening, a political satire show was on, and we felt somehow uneasy: if we didn't laugh at the same things, would a gap of awkwardness open between us if we seemed ungrateful?

Before we went to bed, our hosts asked us where we'd like to sleep, and let us choose between a room where all the mattresses were, and a different room that was empty. Hesitantly, we chose the empty room, thinking that it would be less embarrassing, but they moved all the mattresses to the room we chose and came to sleep with us.

We felt constantly embarrassed, our movements were clumsy, our responses to their questions froze in our mouths, and we felt as if we'd invaded a home that wasn't ours. Suddenly, we were sleeping with a family. We didn't know what was more alien to us—the Arab food, their pile of mattresses, their school—or maybe simply living with a family.

We were relieved to go home, to our Institution, to our wanderings, our life. Every detail of their homes lived in our minds like a short story, like a stage set.

A week after we returned, Netta received a letter from Tamra—one of the boys wrote that he'd fallen in love with her. "I think about your blue eyes and your blond curls all the time," he wrote.

In our junior year, some classes went to religious kibbutzim and moshavim, and some went to a "young kibbutz," which usually meant a different or experimental kibbutz.

We went to Kerem Shalom, the western-most kibbutz in the country, near the Egyptian-Israeli border at Raffiah. The story of Kerem Shalom was like a socialist legend, told to us over and over again by different sources. They said it was a kibbutz that had never become morally corrupt or bourgeois. They said that on Kerem Shalom, everyone swam naked in the pool. They said that on Kerem Shalom, there were spontaneous kibbutz meetings—if something bothered someone, he rang a bell and everyone dropped everything and came running. Nothing was frozen in rules and regulations, or set in stone. As if everything there truly began at the beginning. They said that the members of Kerem Shalom were ideologues who demonstrated against the injustices of the settlers in the Gaza Strip and northern Sinai, organized petitions, and refused to rest until true peace and justice reigned here.

The experimental version of the kibbutz was established in the '60s by a core group known as Gilat (made up of people from well-to-do families), which was the first core group of kibbutz members' children who, like us, were graduates of educational institutions. During the first few years, another group of kibbutz members joined them, and in the following years, two core groups of urban youth who weren't members of youth movements joined them as well. Those core groups—Shalom and Avshalom—became known later for members who had become writers, film producers, designers, editors of books and newspapers.

We arrived at the kibbutz and worked for five days. We all slept together in a sports hall at the far end of the kibbutz. When we arrived, we were told that we hadn't come at a good time, that the kibbutz was in the midst of a great upheaval because several important members had left after another split that had occurred. Nonetheless, they sent someone to the hall to see us after work (wearing blue work clothes, of course; kibbutz ideologues of every stripe, conservatives and experimentalists alike, always wore work clothes when they spoke), to tell us how everything began, and then they took us to observe a kibbutz meeting.

Even though we couldn't really feel the legend in Kerem Shalom, we believed that it existed, and were happy to be there, away from our lives for a week. We told our group mates who'd visited a religious moshav about our experience, and they told us about theirs.

They said that their hosts on the religious moshav were very warm, good people, excellent basketball players and not half bad at soccer. They told us that they slept in their houses, played with them, went to class with them and worked in the citrus orchards with them twice in the middle of the week. But the most interesting thing was the weekend, when they spent the Sabbath with them. The atmosphere was different, they said, when Sabbath began on Friday night. Loud, joyous singing, prayer, and a large, delicious meal. The next day, Saturday, they were invited to a meeting with the rabbi.

Many of our group mates were late to the meeting. They'd fallen asleep. They said that the rabbi managed to work everything that happened into his talk. He used the latecomers, for example, to provide two examples of what proper behavior on the Sabbath should be: The first took place right at the beginning, when the ones who had come on time were already seated and the latecomers rang the bell. The rabbi, half smiling and half shocked, explained that both he and they were forbidden to open the door because that would continue the desecration of the Sabbath, which began with the ringing of the bell.

But after the latecomers somehow managed to enter and saw that there weren't enough chairs for them, the rabbi explained that nothing prevented them from walking the long way back to get more chairs, even if they thought that was strenuous work, which is forbidden on the Sabbath. He explained that there was no connection between physical labor that didn't necessarily desecrate the Sabbath, and work that did.

At night, they slept in pairs or threesomes in their hosts' homes. The rabbi and his wife, who also hosted them in their home, sat with their guests every night and told them so many things that they couldn't remember all of them when they recounted their experiences to us. For instance, the rabbi and his wife told them about the wonders of nida, the tradition of married women sleeping alone during menstruation. Every month, when menstruation was over, a woman became a beautiful bride again.

The high point of all of our Broadening Horizons Weeks was in our senior year. We went to Tel Aviv to see and experience the way people worked in the big city, how the capitalist urbanites exploited the factory workers.

We slept in the Bnei Dan hostel near the Yarkon River in Tel Aviv, and for a week, we worked in factories in Ramat Hayal, which, at the time, was in the industrial area. We worked in the Sinon factory, which made air filters for vehicles, in the Shavit oven factory, owned by Booma Shavit, who was the Chairman of the Industrialists Association, and in the Til Ohn wire and screw factory.

In the factories, we sat at a real production line that seemed to have been leased from the set of Charlie Chaplin's *Modern Times* especially for us.

We started work early in the morning. We took two buses or walked a long way to a different bus stop in order to get there on time. We pestered the workers with questions: How much did they earn? Did they get breaks? Why didn't they organize in order to improve conditions? We were there for a week and left. They worked there for decades.

On the kibbutz, we sang, "We know nothing about taxes and fees/But we know about flowers and trees," and perhaps because they didn't want to make life difficult for us with problems like cash flow or overdraft, we received in advance what they said was the equivalent of a week's wages. No one mentioned overtime, bonuses, vacation days, time clocks, etc.

We worked four or six hours a day so we would have the strength to have afternoon meetings with the urban workers, our brothers in the struggle. No homeroom teachers or *metaplot* came with us on our Broadening Horizons Weeks. We went out to enjoy ourselves at night.

Money wasn't a problem, because we'd received minimum wage for our half-days of work, and we didn't have to buy clothes, pay rent, raise children, pay bills, buy food or pay interest on our overdraft. All the money was invested in bus rides and entertainment.

But instead of being convinced of the rightness of our system, or drawing the workers to it, we were drawn to city life. We went to movies, plays and teahouses. We saw Camus' *The Fall* on the stage with Nico Nitai. We ordered smoked tea. We laughed constantly. Idit adopted a dog, a puppy that was walking along near the factories, and we called her Tsippi. Even though we worked seemingly monotonous jobs in the factories, many unexpected things happened to us there, on the buses and in the hostel. We saw the city and met the sort of people we'd never met before. Everything had flavor. For a week, we forgot our fear that perhaps life had no meaning. We were busy and we laughed all evening. We wanted to go out more and more.

Every summer, when the year at the Institution ended, we detached ourselves from the Shomrat kids, who had been welded to us in the Seagull group, and to the rest of the Institution kids who weren't from Yehiam, the ones from Gaaton and Evron, the ones who were in higher and lower grades than we were—we said goodbye to everyone we loved, or were undecided about whether we loved them or not, because there were no couples from the same kibbutz, only ones made up of boys and girls from different kibbutzim. We knew that we'd be apart for months, and would only see them on a few trips and visits.

In June, right before the summer vacation, we spent a great deal of time together. Maybe because we'd soon be saying goodbye. We bought watermelons and went to the Nahariya beach at night. We swam and talked.

When we came back from the beach, we dreamed that the waves were huge, reaching up to touch the sky, and in the dream, we were shocked but excited, as if we had actually experienced a natural phenomenon in our sleep.

During recesses, we lay on the lawn and stared up at the treetops. The grass was soft, tall and very green—it sparkled. We thought about things. We were happy and unhappy with no connection to what was happening. One moment up, the next down. We talked about the boys we loved or maybe were only attracted to. We closed our eyes and opened them. The sun shone through the leaves. We wanted to know whether attraction and love were the same thing. Hagit explained to us what sexy meant. We wanted to think that anything (including attraction) but love was happening to us; we didn't want to be dependent on the boys, as if they were dragging us, tied to a sled, from now to forever. Being dependent on love was as sweet as love and as bitter as dependence. We were flung from bitterness to sweetness as if from hilltop to hilltop, and in between, a gaping abyss—the grass on which we lay.

Shlomi left class and came to the lawn to call us in for a literature or psychology lesson. We said we'd be right there, in a minute, we're coming. When he went back, we kept talking and forgot. Then it was too late and there was no point in going to class. Shlomi was from Shomrat, and the Shomrat girls said we'd see each other a lot, but every year, things had their own cycles, their own seasons, and in the summer, we worked on the kibbutzim and forgot the rest of the year. We went back to being Narcissus, Anemone, Terebinth and Oak, and for two months, we lived our lives on Kibbutz Yehiam.

15

Every September, we returned to the Educational Institution after two month's summer vacation, during which we worked on our kibbutzim.

From one year to the next, everything became more. In the tenth grade, it was as if we'd moved all at once from thinking to acting, from standing to moving. We no longer exaggerated when we talked about what we did. What we did exaggerated itself. We collided with the world. The world was present, and so were we and what we did.

Love remained intangible, but its results were felt everywhere: Couples walked hand in hand all the time; some girls stayed on their kibbutzim with volunteers, or with boys from their groups, slipping back to the Educational Institution in the morning. There were couples who slept together in the Institution and went back to their beds before the *metaplot* went from room to room waking us up. Some couples walked along the peripheral road that encircled the Institution up to the reservoir, or had sex in the air raid shelters on thin mattresses, or without mattresses at all, or on a blanket outside; some had sex on the beds in their rooms, and sometimes, the others who lived in those rooms were there, lying on the other beds, and sometimes they weren't.

On the afternoons when we didn't work, we wandered or stretched out on the lawn near our classroom in Seagull, or we sat in the basketball court stands, looking beyond the boys playing there, or stared at the ground as we drew imaginary circles on earth and concrete with branches.

"I'm late this month," one of the girls would sometimes say in terror during those moments, as if the words were being pushed out of her mouth against her will. We caught our breath, looked at her for a moment, checked ourselves, not knowing whether it was happening in our bodies or in our friend's, no matter if we'd had sex already or not. As if the power of fear alone could impregnate us with something we'd never known before. What was she saying now, something about herself or about us? How should we reply?

Abortions were arranged by the kibbutzim, not the Institution. On Yehiam, my mother was the nurse, and the abortions were done in Nahariya, with the kibbutz nurse. Anyone who had to go through it, went through it. Once or twice or three times. They said it wasn't a matter of luck, that something could be done to prevent it from happening. But it was a matter of luck too—once or twice or three times.

In the morning, during breaks, we talked with the girls about what love was, and at night, sometimes with the boys. We thought constantly about what love was. We opened and closed our eyes when we talked about it, we looked at the sky or the ground to keep from looking into the eyes of the people who were speaking. We thought they couldn't see anything on us. We hoped they couldn't see anything on us. There was nowhere to hide. We were always in the light—the sunlight in the morning and the lamps at night, in the rooms that four of us shared, one in each corner, where someone was always reading or doing something else with the light on.

Those who didn't want to see or be seen covered their eyes with their hands.

Idit and I wrote to each other constantly. During classes and afterwards. And we were always together anyway. When everything was exaggerated and had become more—we also moved into the same room.

We moved into the room that adjoined our classroom. An open concrete area separated those two rooms from the rest of the long building that contained all the other rooms, the two communal shower rooms (one for boys, one for girls) and the two communal bathrooms we all used. "Our" room was tiny. Until we invaded it, it had been called "the *metapelet*'s room," and it contained a supply of toilet paper as well as tea and sugar for the coffee corner that was right next to it. Once a year, they held a round of homeroom teachers' talks in it. But most of the year, it was empty. The emptiness piqued our interest. We made it habitable and simply moved into it. They couldn't find a clause that would support an objection, and we stayed there.

Later, we opened a teahouse in an empty air raid shelter. We painted it blue, and Idit drew an enormous mural on one of the walls. Using a magic lantern, she projected the original on the wall and for days, she worked on a painting on the blue wall. In the Regional Council building, we found a huge record collection kept there by Arieh, the music teacher from Beit Haemek. We moved the collection to our teahouse. We told each other that if Arieh knew where his classical music records had disappeared to, he might even be happy about it. We made menus listing a variety of teas and announced the opening of our teahouse. People read there, drank tea, listened to Beethoven symphonies from Arieh's collection, and sometimes held meetings of the newsletter or cultural committees there. The teahouse became one of the places to wander to. All the places that weren't locked were also accessible in the evenings—the reading room, the painting room, the music room, the shelters where instrumental groups and singers rehearsed. We wandered from place to place, searching for quiet, searching for noise. Everyone asked, "Where is everyone?"

Idit and I saw signs in everything, as if our eyes kept opening wider and wider until the shadow of hills looked like hills or like valleys to us. We preferred living the signs to living the world. We tried to avoid the world, to keep it at bay behind the door, to prevent any contact between us and it.

Idit studied painting, music and dancing. I read, fasted, abstained and swore oaths. First I stopped eating meat for a week. Then I tried not to eat at all for a few days. Then I stopped talking for a week. When my teachers asked me about that, I handed them a page of explanation I'd written.

We felt that if we isolated things we might understand or know. We wrote down the dreams we had at night, believed that they spoke the truth. We searched for truth as if it were an object we couldn't see in the dark.

When Margalit came to wake us in the morning, I fainted at the end of one of my fasts. She was frightened. She stood at the door to our room and explained to us the world we were trying to avoid. She said that there were people who didn't stop observing things from the outside even after their adolescence, people who never really entered life, and that kept them adolescents ever after they'd become adults. Everyone knows where adolescence begins, she said, but no one knows where it ends.

Yael at the Educational Institution.

Two meters separated Idit and me in our room, and three meters separated my desk from hers in class—she sat diagonally in front of me. And the shorter the distance between us, the longer our letters grew.

We were all children of the system, its students, and we usually became youth movement leaders (the Hashomer Hatzair movement, of course), in the tenth grade. When we were in the ninth grade, the Grove group, which was a grade ahead of us, didn't have enough group leaders, so I became a youth group leader together with Rami, who was already in the tenth grade.

Apart from organizing the activities, which took place once a week in the Nahariya Hashomer Hatzair chapter, Rami and I also went to camps and on trips together. Walking the road to Nahariya with Rami was the continuation of a much longer path, as if we'd walked it together even before we were born, in other landscapes.

Our mothers had known each other back in Budapest, and were already friends there. Later they were in the same Hashomer Hatzair core group, The First of May. Then after the war, each came separately to the same Shuffiya hills, my mother to Yehiam and his to Gaaton.

Rami's parents, along with Rami and his three sisters, came to visit us on Yehiam, and we visited them on Gaaton; we lived two kilometers apart. Rami's older sisters were the same age as my older brothers, and had been in the same groups at the Educational Institution since they were twelve. His sisters played the violin and viola, Rami played the cello and his father and youngest sister also played the violin, so that in almost any situation, they could play a quartet.

When we became youth group leaders together, we discovered that we had both signed out the same library books. The Institution library was open five days a week. It contained thousands of books: textbooks, literary fiction and reference books. All the newest books of fiction fell apart when Rami or I read them the first time. We could also borrow books from the kibbutz libraries, which were even larger. By looking at the lenders card in a book, we could tell who had read it before us.

Rami, Idit and I also loved going to shows, plays and concerts in the Evron hall.

We didn't have to move from where we were. In those days, we were the center of the world, and everyone came to us. Performers toured all the kibbutzim; the culture committees had huge budgets. Kibbutz Evron had a modern hall with excellent acoustics. We saw major singers there, as well as fringe performers who would become major several years later. We could get in to see anything. We heard all the concerts and saw all the plays and dance performances.

When Rami and I completed our year as youth group leaders, I continued to speak to him in my mind. At first, I thought it was out of habit, that we used to talk like that while walking to our group activities in Nahariya, on the trips and on our way to the youth camps. Then I thought that it might be because of our families' years of friendship.

But it was something else, something that persisted. As if the previous order of my life were betraying me, refusing to return to what it had been.

Idit and I wrote each other and talked about Rami too, asking why it was that the girls never loved the boys who loved them and vice versa. Rami asked Idit to be his girlfriend when we were in the eighth grade, and Tali, of the Grove group, would occasionally come to a Seagull girl with a proposal from a Grove boy to be his girlfriend. Idit met with Rami then and told him that she wasn't interested. And she didn't become interested later on either. As far as she was concerned, it belonged to the past.

But I grew entrapped in my thoughts of him, as if they had become a giant labyrinth, a hidden city, an entire world. I began to see signs in everything: After all, we borrowed the same library books and always went to the same performances; after all, Romeo and Juliet could have been Ram and Yael, like in Itzhak Salkinson's old translation of the play, which we had both taken out of the library; after all, we could have been neighbors living two kilometers apart not only in Gaaton and Yehiam, but in Buda and Pest, and instead of swimming in the Gaaton River, we could have swum in the freezing water of the Danube like my mother had, like perhaps his mother had.

At night, I dreamt about Rami. Simple dreams, with no plot complications. As if a plot would only conceal him. The melody of the dream was sweet, like the absence of worry. And while the plot was so clear at night, I didn't understand it in the morning.

When none of that passed, I wrote him an eleven-page letter. I wrote that I didn't know whether I loved him or just thought about him, whether I spoke to him or just to an imaginary figure I could direct my inner speech at. (Sometimes I thought of him as a huge cat because he had soft, almost white hair and his eyes were as green as a cat's. He always walked quietly, stepping high, as if he were drawn by the air, not the ground, and because of the total silence he walked within, he would always appear in unexpected places.)

Rami received the letter, and in the Institution's dining hall, when we were stacking dishes in the large stainless steel sinks, he came over to me. We arranged to meet at eight that night at the regular place, the bus stop, where the circular paths around the Institution began. We walked to the Regional Council building. Flowers grew there and the grass was green and soft. Rami said that I was going around in circles, that everything was simple. "The complication is only in your mind," he said. "Love is as simple as knowledge," he said.

At the end of my first notebook of dreams, I wrote about the image of Rami that appeared constantly in my dreams:

> Rami—my relationship to him is not very clearly defined. We were youth group leaders together, and at some point, I was sure that I loved him. Maybe sometimes now too. Even after writing to him and seeing him, I still feel the same way, that I don't know. Zohar appears in my dreams a lot, and always with Rami. I think that Zohar in my dreams is a symbol of what I'd like to continue being, because on one hand, Zohar is like me, from Seagull and from Yehiam, but on the other, the relationship between Rami and Zohar is not "suspicious" because they're both boys, and also because Zohar has a good reason to be with Rami—they both play in the same music group. Back when we saw each other a lot, because we were group leaders together, we didn't need a reason or an excuse, and we didn't need to define our relationship exactly, love or friendship. It just was.

All that time, Rami loved Idit. He asked her to be his girlfriend twice. The first time, when we were in the eighth grade, and the second time, he went to see her in the piano room when she was playing and tried to persuade her. That was several months after the long letter I wrote to him and after he and I walked to the Regional Council building, and at the same time, Idit and I were writing to each other about how the girls never loved the boys who loved them and vice versa.

Back then, so many things happened in a few months. The ones who loved, no longer loved, and the ones who didn't love—loved. But between Rami and Idit, nothing changed during those two years.

I was sick, and back on Yehiam because when we were unwell or pregnant, when something went wrong, we left the Institution and stayed on the kibbutz until we were healthy again. Even when we were on our kibbutzim, Idit and I wrote to each other every day. (There were no phones in our parents' houses, and of course, not in the Institution either. On Yehiam, there was one phone available to the members. They would turn off the meter after they used it, and write in pencil the number of calls they made. That was only so the kibbutz could keep track—no one was charged.) We sent the letters we wrote with our teachers, who traveled to the Institution and back every day.

Idit wrote to me:

This is how I felt this morning/or: The Night of the 15th …/or: The Fall

You'll understand in a minute what all those titles hint at, and when you get well, I'll tell you everything and I hope it won't make you sick again. I keep thinking that you know what happened yesterday and I really don't have to tell you, but…

Silence…

Yesterday, Rami asked me to be his girlfriend. In a totally egotistical way. He said: "I know that things can't get any worse for me than they are now (time did not make it better). I've been stuck in the same place for two years," and he thinks and asks me to be his girlfriend, no matter where it leads, just as long as it leads somewhere.

He tried to get back on his feet, but fell again—hopeless. He sees himself as a different person after those two years, even when it comes to me. He wants to get to know me and know how things will end up... He said that he knows I'm the one who has to make the effort, but he's asking me to make it because he thinks he has no other choice now. It never occurred to him that the answer would be "no," and he also said that he couldn't consider the possibility of a no, but he knew about Micah the whole time.

Okay, that's more or less what I remember of what he said, but I'll also tell you what I said.

I hope that this isn't making you mad... He's smart and all that, but he's NOT FOR ME.

I explained to him, and in a nice way (as nice as such a thing can be) that I don't feel anything for him, and that if I said yes, it would only be OUT OF PITY, and not because I feel anything for him. It would go against my feelings, and not worth the effort because what does being boyfriend and girlfriend mean? It means doing things WITH SOMEONE, not TO SOMEONE (I'm really starting to feel like it's pissing me off already).

He kept saying, think it over, think it over...

What is there to think about here, except the way to say no? I explained my position clearly. I told him that I have someone else in mind, and it doesn't matter whether he exists or not, but it's definitely not him (Rami). There's a lot I don't remember, I sat there like a prisoner, I didn't feel good talking to him and it made me sad to think of how the girls never love the boys who love them and vice versa…

When I left, I decided that I definitely did not agree with anything that happened!!! I know that I would never do anything that was THE DIRECT OPPOSITE OF WHAT I FEEL, whether it's out of pity or obligation.

Whatever is inside me, whatever I have to give, I'm saving to give to a person I feel something for, or someone I know I want…

Yael, think about it a little, and it doesn't matter if you only heard my side of things. Always remember that Idit really doesn't love Rami.

Okay, enough about this, I'm sick of it and of the whole mess.

It was nice in our room. Too bad you didn't come yesterday because I brought some great chocolate milk.

Why is someone I'm not interested in interested in me and vice versa?

Idit

GET WELL VERY VERY SOON

In June, right before the summer vacation between the tenth and eleventh grades, we all wandered together before going our separate ways to Yehiam and Shomrat. We went to the beach in Nahariya at night, and bought watermelons on the way.

We talked about the poem we learned with Shlomi, "Parting," by

Gabriel Priel, the poem he'd brought from the Theory of Literature course he was taking in Tel Aviv. Idit liked her paintings to have some connection to poems, but not as illustrations. It was something else. She had the sketch of a new painting that she called the black sketch. She called the painting "Parting," like the poem:

She sat facing me and her eyes
Were brown from the coffee
Tortured from my body
As I tried to tell her
All the green things I had learned.
She surely did not listen:
She was trapped
In a cage of strangenesses,
Or walking down a street
That refused to meet
Another street.

Yet I know that her eyes turned briefly green,
Seeing a garden praying in the rain.
The dagger seemed thus to be pulled
From the brown valleys
And great stars
On the roads
Protected a small tranquility:
It will not reach me.

We rehearsed for the end-of-year play, and on one of those nights, I wrote in my dreams notebook:

I dreamt that people say Idit is always in Rami's room and I ask her: If Rami asks you to be his girlfriend NOW, would you say yes? And she laughs and says: Why not?

Below every dream, I wrote about all sorts of things that really happened and were connected to the dream. I gave them the permanent title "Yosef's Column." Under that dream, I wrote:

Idit and I were talking about something today, and we bumped into Esti on the sidewalk. She said she was going to a rehearsal in Rami's room. And without being able to explain it exactly, I felt as if something changed in Idit, that inside her, she suddenly turned toward Rami, and I felt terrible there, on the sidewalk, as if a huge hole had suddenly opened in the ground. That's why this dream is totally accurate in terms of my feelings, when Idit answers, why not. I hope the dream isn't a prophecy…

Idit was always painting, but that summer, in the Educational Institution, before we went back to Yehiam and Shomrat for summer vacation, her paintings began to speak, to spill off the canvas into the room. Then the hints began to add up, the signs began to add up, as if her love for Rami was only the last link in a chain that was larger than her, larger than Rami, larger than all of us.

Even though Idit and I wrote to each other constantly and were together constantly, it was difficult to know exactly when things happened, when words changed to deeds. She became an artist all at once. And it happened. At the same time. Rami and Idit became a couple.

16

The Hashomer Hatzair commune at 6 Hahavazelet Street in Ramat Gan was our first city address. That address wasn't supposed to mark the beginning of city life, but was rather another stage of kibbutz life.

In an arrangement between the Hashomer Hatzair and the army, the army allocated a quota of up to 120 young kibbutz members who could postpone their army service for one year, the "thirteenth year" after their twelve years of school, to do volunteer work in various cities. Or they could learn Arabic for a year on Givat Haviva. Back then, you had to be gifted and curious to study Arabic seriously for a year. We had no matriculation certificate and we hardly learned anything in the Educational Institution.

During that thirteenth year, we were youth group leaders in the city chapters of the movement and were supposed to inspire young urbanites to join kibbutzim. Who would be assigned where was determined by lottery. Before receiving assignments in the cities, each of us wrote down the names of two places we preferred. I asked for Jerusalem or Tel Aviv. I was relieved to be placed in Ramat Gan, outside of Tel Aviv. Since everything was always determined by some arcane method, by some committee that weighed desire against need, and equality against other considerations, we were used to the idea that it could always be much worse than what we wanted, much further removed from what we hoped.

Boaz, Gil and I were assigned to the Ramat Gan chapter. At 25, Gil was older than Boaz and me, and a combat officer and an outstanding worker in the banana plantation before he went to the Ramat Gan chapter as an emissary. Our movement, Hashomer Hatzair, seemed to be afraid to stay in one place, and its lexicon was comprised of words related to action and motion: it was active by virtue of its name—"movement"—and those who were occasionally called to serve in its ranks, in rotation, were called "activists" and "emissaries." All our words alluded to the future: momentum, action and missions, but we always remained in the same spot.

That thirteenth year was the first time we were taken out of the group we were born into on Yehiam, and the group from Shomrat that had been welded onto us in the Educational Institution.

Until we were eighteen, we'd been together constantly in classes, at work, socially and in the movement. The Hashomer Hatzair kibbutzims' perception of the group was based on the belief that educating for socialism begins right at birth and is not imposed from above by adults (that would recreate the coercive parent-child relationship, and would lose its egalitarianism). Everything happened in what is known as the peer group, a group of equals, without parents and older or younger siblings, without hierarchies.

The group was always and everywhere—24 hours a day, from waking until sleeping, from the babies' house to the end of the twelfth grade.

The group wasn't a class, and schoolwork wasn't the point. The classroom and schoolwork were only part of the means. Sports, music, hikes, scouting, work—they were additional means to realize our creativity and to achieve socialism. Each of us helped the other where he was weak.

The aim was not to create identical people, but to create the equality of opportunity that would allow each member of the group to grow to his fullest.

The commune where we lived was a two-story private house, attached on both sides. It was old and dusty, and although we didn't decorate or prettify it, we still felt it was too much for us.

The three of us got along well. We'd learned to be considerate from the beginning, living our lives among a group of equals. Now we were a very small group of three living in comfortable conditions, each in his own room.

The Ramat Gan chapter of Hashomer Hatzair was small and existed in the shadow of a huge troop of Scouts. There was only one group for each age, and that was only if one of us managed to recruit enough young people to form a group. Sometimes the groups dissolved within weeks or days. A few new members chose Hashomer

A Hashomer Hatzair meeting.

Hatzair and stayed for a few years. The others came by chance, wandered in to check out what was happening.

In that thirteenth year, we attended theoretical seminars in how to be youth movement leaders. We learned how to lead city children in a way that didn't make them feel they were being lectured to or told what to do "from above." The activities were supposed to create "value actualization," and illustrate the Hashomer Hatzair values of cooperation and mutual assistance in action. It was called "the uniting of action and message." Izhar ben Nahum, from Kibbutz Beit Zera, illustrates this:

> If you are guiding a group in Tel Aviv, for example, you can go to the Yarkon River and talk about fishing, what the essence of that profession is, and why people choose that occupation and not a different one. From that you can con-

tinue on to a more social discussion on a breakdown of different occupations, about the rich and the poor, about what ownership of the means of production is, and what happens when someone like us goes to the Yarkon, catches fish and eats them, and the next day, he goes back to the river and sees that there is a fence, and some real estate magnate who bought the Yarkon tells him: "Now if you want to fish, you have to pay me," and employs him as a salaried fisherman. The hard-working fisherman fishes all day for a few pennies, while the real estate magnate who bought the Yarkon River receives the money for selling the fish. And then you explain to your group about the ownership of the means of production, and from there, the way to Marx is short. You'll see that everything moves easily, from the simple to the complex, because the activity began with a walk to the Yarkon and a conversation about fishing.

Gil and Boaz divided our daily tasks in the commune by hours. They wrote the hours in four numbers, which made the schedules seem realistic and authoritative, devoid of wasted time. Between 07:00 and 08:30, get up, eat breakfast and clean the commune. Between 10:00 and 11:00, go to Blich High School to recruit new members. Then get various permits from the municipality, prepare our activities for that evening and so on.

We bought on credit in the grocery store next door to the commune. The group leaders we took over from told us not to forget to check the bills once a month before we paid. The young members used to come to the commune to talk to us about problems with schoolwork, or problems they had with each other, who they were in love with, or just to pass the time. They said that they loved the activities even if they weren't always interested in everything we talked about. We went to their homes to persuade their parents to let them go on hikes the movement organized.

We believed that nature hikes taught things that could not be learned in years of everyday life. They provided a look at relationships and worlds different from the ones in classrooms, at social evenings or work. There were people to help those who found it difficult to get from one riverbank to the other, people who cooked soup on the campfire, and still others who gathered wood for the fire. The group leaders were with their groups twenty-four hours a day, lived the same lives as they did, ate with them and slept in sleeping bags on the ground with them.

In scouting seminars and in preparation for those trips, Yonatan ben Nahum, brother of Izhar from Kibbutz Beit Zera, taught us how to build a shelter in the bushes for sleeping at night, and how to survive on energy-rich natural foods. We learned that, at night, when you can't see well and background noise is greatly decreased, you can sharpen your aural sense and utilize it to its fullest to help you feel safer and more comfortable in the dark.

In the third grade we were already going out once a week for a full day's walk with our teacher, Rivka, instead of learning in class.

Sometimes Eliezer A. went with us to deepen our knowledge of nature, to sharpen our observation of flowers and plants, to teach us to identify cassia and poterium plants and to distinguish between pine mushrooms and poisonous mushrooms. Rivka used to say that we climbed beautifully, like ibexes; Eliezer said that we were mountain children and we shouldn't whine when we step on thorns, because mountain children don't cry.

In the Educational Institution, Hagit and I were terrified on youth movement hikes. We dreamt every night that we were hovering above the chasms that the boys helped us to cross as we clutched the rocky protrusions, but the rocks fell from under our feet and we plunged down, down, down. When we were on the hike, we wanted it to end. When we slept, we wanted to wake up. But after being tossed between the nightmare and the view that came after it on the trip, when our sense of having been constantly rescued had passed, we felt as if we had touched the star-strewn sky and had smelled the earth—the stars adorned our sleeping bags, we loved the campfire. We moved from extreme to extreme, as if inside us, we were moving from desert heat to Alpine cold.

Back home, after the trips, we suddenly recalled certain moments without knowing why. Sometimes, things that had been difficult, frightening and unbearable there, later became something else, as if we remembered the escape from the moment, and not the moment itself, and other times, at home, we were more frightened than we had been at the particular moment when we were stuck on a huge rock. The hikes were unlike anything else in terms of their difficulty and the richness of the nature that came to us from unexpected places, as if it spilled from the trees, the bushes, the earth, the vegetation, and from ourselves. Long after we returned, moments from the hikes leaped out at us on the sidewalk, as we went about our daily lives, like bits of a dream or fragments of a different life.

We used to take our dirty laundry to our kibbutzim every other Sunday when we went to work there for two days, and bring the clean laundry back, along with avocados and toilet paper. Boaz's father occasionally brought us boxes of food when he came to Tel Aviv with the activists' car that was at his disposal.

Once, twice or three times a week, Boaz and I took the number 61 bus to Tel Aviv, where we met up with group leaders in the North Tel Aviv chapter. We bought books, went to movies and art gallery exhibits. We were surrounded by the city and city people. We were like tourists in our own world, in a no man's land between city and kibbutz, which had been "lent" to us for a year.

Boaz, Gil and I came from totally different parts of the country: Boaz was from the Negev in the south, Gil from the Jordan Valley in the east, and I was from the Western Galilee in the north. Nevertheless, Boaz and I had known each other's faces and names even before that year in Ramat Gan. We had seen the kids in the other educational institutions, who were exactly like us, on youth movement trips during vacations, and mainly at the theoretical seminars we all attended on Givat Haviva.

At the end of our senior year, we met on Givat Haviva at a seminar on Zionism and Judaism. The subjects of the seminars had been similar throughout the years, the lecturers remained, and only the audience changed. We had various group discussions on Zionism, Israeliness and Judaism, on what it meant to be Jewish in our times, and also on what was called "current political problems": We heard Gershon Shafat from the Gush Emunim settlements, who gave a lecture on the Gush's political position, and we heard Meir Pail on Israel's various conceptions of security and on a functional, territorial compromise.

We even knew—or seemed to know—Gil, who was several years older than us, from his similar past in the Hashomer Hatzair kibbutzim: We all grew up in the Children's Society on remote kibbutzim. On holidays, we all sang the songs written by members of Hashomer Hatzair kibbutzim with the purpose of bringing new content to the Jewish holidays.

In the first grade, on the Shavuot holiday (which we called the festival of the first fruits in order to emphasize its agricultural aspect in the celebration of the first harvests), and after the women had mounted the stage with the new babies born that year, we stood in a row on the stage, each of us with a fluttering dove in our hands.

We tried not to drop the doves as we stood in front of the entire kibbutz, concentrating on the complicated lyrics and wonderful melody that rose like a cry of longing (words by Dov Shai, one of the founders of Kibbutz Ramat Hashofet, and music by Izhar Yaron, who left Tel Aviv to join Kibbutz Ein Hashofet):

Behold, behold up in the sky:
The clouds among the blue.
Set off and carry, white-winged birds,
A message—hopeful, true.

Fly off, fly off, doves pearly white,
Fly with a trumpeting of light.
Our brothers wait for you, farewell,
Return in haste with ringing bells.

When the signal was given at the end of the song, we all released the doves to the sky, and from there, to our brothers on all the kibbutzim.

Every other week, on Sundays and Mondays, we each went to our own kibbutz to work there, and every other week, on those same days, we attended a seminar called School on Givat Haviva.

We reached Givat Haviva around noon on Sunday, and first of all, we read the agenda that was pinned on the bulletin board. The agenda was organized with the same system used by Gil and Boaz: Every hour was written in four numbers, followed by a colon and then the details. Arrival and assigning of rooms, lunch, afternoon rest, four o'clock refreshments, supper, party (or a movie or night swimming in the pool), and the next day breakfast, ten o'clock refreshments, lunch and departure. The lecturers arrived between the meals, some of them intellectuals from the surrounding kibbutzim who were brought in by the "Central Leadership" for an hour or two, clad in blue work clothes, of course.

While it wasn't written on the agenda, at almost every School seminar there was a soccer game between us, youth movement group leaders, and the "Arabists," the ones who were studying Arabic on Givat Haviva for a year. If Hanan, a group leader from Beit Shean who played soccer for Hapoel Beit Shean, was there, our group won. If he wasn't there, the Arabists won, even though there were a lot fewer of them and they excelled in the classroom, not on the soccer field. They won not only because of their home turf advantage (they lived on Givat Haviva all year round), but also because of the hard work of their goalkeeper, Ranen. He was methodical about keeping balls out of the net, as if that was something they taught at the seminar on Givat Haviva.

Givat Haviva was the temple of our secular gods. The secretariat of the Kibbutz Artzi held its meetings there, and the Executive Committee held its famous conferences there, with Yaakov Hazan, Meir Yaari and Haike Grossman. Givat Haviva was established in July 1949 as a center for seminars and lectures. The center was named after the parachutist, Haviva Reik, a member of Kibbutz Maanit who was executed by the Nazis in 1944.

Our system believed that everything could be taught and learned in seminars, because the Hashomer Hatzair believed that we were bringing about the socialist revolution. History is not a collection of stories and associations, but rather an organized, scientific process. One thing leads to another, which leads to another. We scorned miracles, randomness and religion. If we possess knowledge, on the one hand, and are persuasive on the other, success was certain.

On Givat Haviva, we all studied everything: courses in Arabic, seminars for group leaders of all ages, School for thirteenth-year group leaders, seminars for the various committee coordinators, for recently discharged soldiers, for singles, kitchen workers and barn workers, and even a drug seminar aimed at coming up with ideas on how to prevent smoking and drug use on the kibbutzim. Also invited to those seminars were drug users, who always promised that they'd stopped smoking (before or after the secretariat called the police to the kibbutz). Later, they said that they could never smoke in such an idyllic place. Givat Haviva was paradise for all its students.

Givat Haviva was the perfect kibbutz setting, without being a kibbutz: No cow barns, no fields, no tractors or power ladders, no work scheduler, no work and no members. There was a dining hall there, like on any kibbutz, and a swimming pool like on any kibbutz, and eternally green lawns like on any kibbutz, only in better condition, because no one trod on them. Givat Haviva was like a huge dollhouse, a sweet dream with no cracks in it, because it had no reality, no concrete world. A school for a life of socialism with no life to ruin it, no people. The only people who lived there were the lecturers and seminar students, who usually came for a few days or a week.

The Arabists studied Arabic in the Jewish-Arab Center for Peace established in 1963 on Givat Haviva. The purpose of the Center, according to the Givat Haviva website, is:

> …to bring Jews and Arabs in Israel closer and to educate for mutual understanding and partnership between the two peoples…The Center values humanism and equality of all peoples. It therefore strives to be a key element towards achieving true democracy in Israel, characterized by civil equality between Jewish and Palestinian Israeli citizens. Through the encouragement of social and cultural pluralism, the Center believes regional peace and reconciliation can be achieved.

Our statements of intention were always written in the future tense, which is why they always remained untouched, fresh, evergreen, like the lawns on Givat Haviva, as pristine as the peace doves we all released into the air simultaneously in our first grade harvest celebration.

At the end of that thirteenth year, after delaying life by a year or serving as emissaries of the movement, Gil returned to the Beit Zera banana plantation and to reserve duty as a combat officer.

Until peace came, the Arabists—those who had studied Arabic in the interest of peace—listened in on the Arabs in wartime or during preparations for war. Since they were now fluent in Arabic after a year of intensive study, most of them were recruited into the Intelligence Corps. Some went into the prisoner interrogation unit. A number of the Arab lecturers on Givat Haviva had served in that unit or were former members of the General Security Services.

The brotherhood of peoples and socialism always took place in the future. Our brief past and the ongoing present served as the army's spearhead.

Boaz couldn't decide where to go in the army: the elite combat unit or the pilots course. On our last night in the commune, the three of us weighed the pros and cons of the two possibilities. Gil said that they were both good, and that it's well known that only a few complete the pilots course. So if he didn't make the grade, he could join the elite combat unit. On the con side of the pilots course, I said that it bothered me that there was no real reason the cadets could only go home on leave every three weeks during a two-year course, leaving on Friday and returning Saturday, the next day, and not on Sunday, like everyone else. But giving so little time off, and so infrequently, is probably deliberate, so that the world that exists in the thoughts of the cadets slowly fades and they're one hundred percent there, in the course, totally dedicated. "Yes," Boaz said, "and so that people won't remember this place, or other places like it." We all were carried away on a momentary wave of missing our dusty commune and each other, even though we were still there.

Gil laughed and said to Boaz and me: "Guys, I knew you were a couple from the first night."

We weren't a couple. We went back to our beds early every morning so that Gil wouldn't see us when he went upstairs to shower at 6:30 in the morning. But the first night, Boaz fell asleep in my bed.

The city people always asked us if we slept together when we lived in the same room, boys and girls together, with no adults present, until we were eighteen. A *metapelet* once said to Eyal and me, when the three of us were standing at the Institution bus stop, that the kibbutz had even managed to change sexuality, that there was no sexual tension among the boys in the group. Opinions vary on that issue. "It's a fact," we always answered the city people's questions politely, "that not even a single couple came out of the group. It would have been like incest. It was taboo."

We learned not to reveal what happened in the Institution and later. Not because it was forbidden or allowed, but rather because we were always surrounded by people who knew us, both on the kibbutz and in the Institution. We felt as if the outsiders' eyes of the witnesses would know something about which we still hadn't formed an opinion, that the witness' interpretation would always precede every action.

We communicated with notes and letters to keep from being exposed. We wrote to each other all the time, even when only a few dozen meters separated us and our building from the other groups' buildings. At night, we slipped letters under doors and under pillows and between the pages of books. On the envelopes, we wrote diagonally, in red pen: "Please don't come to see me tonight," meaning exactly the opposite: "Please come to see me tonight." Sometimes, we didn't know whether we loved people so we could have someone to be with, or so we could write and wait for letters. We fell in love with letter writing.

In the commune, we each had a room to ourselves, no roommates, one in each corner. Nonetheless, Boaz and I squeezed together in the same room. We got into each other's single beds just as we did in the Children's Society after the *metapelet* had gone and the fear stirred by the bedtime stories (or on the contrary, by life) hovered in the corridor, threatening to spill over into our rooms. Now that Gil was on the bottom floor and we were alone on the top floor, we slept together and told each other stories from books and poems, from plays that we wrote.

On our last night in the commune, after Gil said that he knew we were a couple from the first night, and after the three of us sat around an invisible campfire in the living room with its Formica furniture and drank instant coffee and talked about the year that had been, Gil went to his room and we slept in Boaz's room. Boaz said that someone from Kibbutz Degania had told him that after Degania had split into the country's first kibbutzim, Degania Aleph and Degania Bet, there was no communal sleeping; the children slept in their parents' houses. The family was very important there, and the *kevutza* ("group," which is what they called the kibbutz) was considered equally important, but not more so. Debates on communal vs. family sleeping took place on all the Valley kibbutzim.

One day, the poet Leah Goldberg came to visit and lecture on Kibbutz Afikim, in the Jordan Valley, the kibbutz adjacent to Degania, and spent the night. That night, she wrote two children's poems that she dedicated to the children of Afikim (the dedication appears in the book *What Do the Does Do?*).

On Afikim, like on all of our kibbutzim, and unlike Degania, the children slept in the children's houses. There, Leah Goldberg wrote "Evening Opposite the Gilad," her feelings about communal sleeping. She took pity on the mother who had lost her son, and in her poem, returned him to her. We read the story of that lullaby to each other as if it were a late lullaby for us:

So heavy are the trees,
The fruit weighs down the boughs,
It is the hour of peace,
When the children fall asleep.

Down to the valley a tender lamb
Descends from Gilead,
A sheep bleats in her pen –
It is her tiny son gone lost.

To mother's lap the lamb returns,
There in the pen he sleeps,
The sheep she kisses him,
And then his name she speaks.

Among the branches hides the night,
And Gilead's prophet goes,
Into the valley silently
To watch the children doze.

To mother's lap the lamb returns,
There in the pen he sleeps,
The sheep she kisses him,
And then his name she speaks.

The next morning, the delegation of the next year's thirteenth-years assigned to Ramat Gan arrived. We brought them up to speed, showed them Blich High School, the building where activities were held and the grocery store where we bought on credit. They also gave us their opinions on the elite combat unit vs. the pilots course. Boaz chose the pilots course.

17

On October 27, 1980, a powerful earthquake shook the ground in several settlements that sat on a rift previously unknown to geologists: Kibbutz Yehiam, in the western Galilee hills and the epicenter of the quake; the Gaaton River, which crosses the city of Nahariya, and overflowed its banks, deluging the tourist horse-drawn carriages, their drivers and passengers; Oshrat, the Educational Institution on Kibbutz Evron attended by the children of Yehiam, Gaaton and Shomrat, the place where 180 teenaged boys and girls went to school, slept, lived and ate from the beginning of the seventh grade to the end of the twelfth; Haifa's lower city, especially Haatzmaut Street, where the Kibbutz Movement accounting offices were located, next door to Café Eva which served coffee in glass mugs; the upscale green Carmel area, where concerts were held and where the best psychologists, orthopedists and orthodontists were located, specialists to whom all the kibbutz children with special problems were sent; 6 Havatzelet Street in Ramat Gan, where the Hashomer Hatzair commune was located; and an armored corps base in the Jordan Valley.

The earthquake was also felt on Gaaton, the kibbutz located only two kilometers from the epicenter in Yehiam; on Kibbutz Kabri, which the yellow Regional Council bus passed to take the Yehiam and Gaaton children to their studies and their lives in the Oshrat Educational Institution on Kibbutz Evron; on Givat Haviva, where everyone was always occupied with one seminar or the other on the evergreen lawns, seeking to make a better world; and in fact, on all the kibbutzim throughout the length and breadth of the country.

There were no casualties and no property damage.

There were several moments of shock, during which people froze in place where they were standing, walking or sitting: On Kibbutz Yehiam, you couldn't tell which of the people frozen in place were Hungarian or French, workers or idlers. In Nahariya, you couldn't tell whether they were doctors or employees of the Carlton Hotel. On Evron, almost everyone seemed trapped in their vehicles, whether it was a bicycle or a car. In Haifa, two Carmelit trains squealed to a stop, the train that climbed the Carmel and the one that descended it. Both were stuck between the stations that led back and forth to and from the central Carmel and Paris Square in the lower city, and not in the stations themselves. In the Hashomer Hatzair Ramat Gan commune, the flames of the ever-present kerosene-doused banner suddenly died. In the Jordan Valley, soldiers froze with weapons in hand, or in the middle of outfitting a tank. The armored battalion stopped moving. It was a crushing, but shining moment, a moment when people received the respect they deserved for their simple, remarkable work, for being here, for their struggle to live and function like all living creatures, like an ant, like a tree. A moment when justice fell upon the earth without warning, and all the dreary, monotonous work was seen as a life's work; a moment when everyone in the world was equal, similar to our compassion for the people of Pompeii, for example, compassion for people in parallel universes, for what we had never been, what we would never be. Similar to the way we wonder at human skeletons in science museums.

There was life here, there were people here. Their hearts beat, their blood flowed, they walked, they gathered, they cooked. There were traces here of men who walked upright and weren't monkeys. There was life, and also death.

It was all an illusion that lasted for only a few moments. Just an illusion. There was no nightmarish death of the kind I always feared. No one froze in place. It was I who cracked.

It was I who cracked, and that's why I was discharged from the army for psychiatric reasons, with two sets of discharge papers—one blue and one gray. The blue was given to me by the induction center officer, who typed it on a typewriter, his hands shaking with anger, after he said to me: "You don't understand, this is a document that will hurt you your whole life. Think about it again, think about your future. You're a smart girl; you're going to screw up your life. It can't be that someone with a brain like yours will be walking around with blue discharge papers."

It's a fact, Mr. Kindhearted Officer. You tried so nicely, really, really nicely, who would have believed it, such kindness in the middle of all that authoritarianism, but it wasn't about the future, it was about the past and the present. The ongoing present. The endlessly ongoing present. That's what I thought, but I stammered apologetically: "I don't know, I'm sure it'll be fine. Thank you, don't worry."

On the outside, the blueness already symbolized someone who was not part of the norm, and on the inside, the code sentence read: "Has been found unsuitable to serve."

A week later, I received gray discharge papers that had been sent to Yehiam by mail, with one of the digits of my identity number wrong. The gray, regular discharge papers had been sent to me by that officer without any request from me, without any benefit to himself, and he even typed a rank on it that was three ranks higher than the private I had been when discharged, and included high praise from my superior officers about how well I carried out the tasks I had been given. Those papers he sent me, without signing his name on them, reflected nothing about me. They were a reflection of him, of a man of good will.

But in the induction center, as I tried to concentrate on the list of things I had to do, I wasn't the least bit concerned about the blue papers that had upset him so much.

Since the discharge was unexpected and happened quickly, I was called to the center on the boys' discharge day. While another soldier handling the discharge procedure, trying to sound authoritative, announced which items of clothing had to be returned and thrown on the long table in front of us, I tried to match his rhythm as best I could. Two pairs of pants, he ordered, and I threw down my Dacron dress pants and regular uniform pants. New model uniforms, he said, and I threw down a skirt. Sweater, and I threw down a tunic. The procedure seemed to be identical to all the other military ceremonies and texts, and it was hard to tell that this time, the gear was rotating in the opposite direction. A moment later, I was free. Tossed into the unformatted, post-army world.

I was discharged after eleven months. I had spent most of my army service in an armored corps battalion in the Jordan Valley. There were religious soldiers there from *yeshivas*[10] that had an arrangement with the army, as well as secular ones. There were soldiers from kibbutzim, moshavim and cities. Rich and poor. It was winter there, untamed nature, intoxicating red-yellow-purple blossoming, and endless mud.

There, I had been alone for the first time. After nineteen years of talking, seeing and living only in a group of people who grew up like me, I came to a place where I didn't know anyone, without the spoken language and body language needed to talk to strangers. I began to learn a new language, translated, as if there were an echo to whatever I said to strangers, as if I were hearing my effort from outside myself.

In the armored corps battalion in the Jordan Valley, we hardly did anything. We made toast on heaters, like in the Educational Institution. There, we toasted the bread on kerosene heaters, and in the battalion, on electric heaters. We used to turn the heaters over in the girls' barracks and place slices of challah on the back of them.

---

[10] A religious Jewish high school focusing on the study of traditional texts.

The army was kid stuff for us, the kibbutz girls. Our basic training had been much harder. And so had the dining hall shifts. We already knew how to work, our hearts had been broken a long time ago, our rites of passage had taken place hundreds of years ago.

In the armored corps battalion in the Jordan Valley, I started smoking in the intensive Hungarian style that was in my genes, with Amit, a city boy, the battalion operations sergeant, and someone you could talk to about books and movies. I started right off with a pack a day, one cigarette after another, to get through the emptiness, to embellish it.

City people liked to visit kibbutzim. We hated their visits. We were embarrassed by the double translation. "Who's that?" the kibbutz members would ask. Sometimes with a look, sometimes in actual words, sometimes behind our backs. Ah, nothing, no one, we'd reply or evade. Sometimes we'd leave the visitors in our rooms and bring them their food there, to avoid answering questions.

Amit's visit fell on Independence Day. How would I stand there, in that U-shaped formation that allowed all of us to see the Memorial Day military parade that led into Independence Day, that same U-shaped formation that kept everyone visible? Everyone saw everyone else. There was no way to hide in the second row. How would I translate for him "Kibbutz, attention!" and then "Kibbutz, at ease!"—military orders spoken in Adam's booming bass voice? How would I translate Gilad Flash's trumpet on the dining hall roof, and then the readings, and between them, the terrible, emotional moment when Haim, our group mate Ronen's brother, read out the names of our members who had been killed? How would I explain to him about the children in their white shirts and the Everlasting

Red pins? And how we all go up to the fortress, the celebrations, the fireworks, the enormous flaming banners?

Amit insisted on not staying in the room. He stood beside me. He roared with laughter and enjoyed every moment (whispered a question to me in the middle: "Why have a military parade on a kibbutz?") I didn't answer him, I wanted him to melt away or fall into a sprinkler pit, to disappear one way or the other.

A new soldier was assigned to the armored corps battalion where I served in the Jordan Valley. He sat next to the headquarters sheds—a delicate young man, a kind of short-haired version of Che Guevara—and every night, accompanied by his guitar, he sang the Beatles "Nothing's gonna change my world" with religious fervor. I'd seen weird sights like that in the army before, and the volunteers on the kibbutz had also sung that song in harmony, but our unusual commander explained to me: "It's a protest."

"Against what?" I asked.

"Against serving in the occupied territories," the commander replied, maybe quoting the new soldier.

"They're sending him from here to the occupied territories?" I asked.

He looked at me in astonishment. We'd had many conversations before that, during which he tried to sway me with all sorts of facts. He was a different kind of commander, one who'd already traveled in the Far East when he was called up and pressured into "returning and contributing a little more to the army," in the kibbutz terminology commonly used by the military. "We need people like you," and all the other arguments aimed straight at the conscience. He returned for a limited time to command an armored corps battalion in the Jordan Valley.

The geographical issue hadn't come up in our previous conversations. He said slowly: "This is the occupied territories."

Only then did I realize that the battalion I'd been serving in for six months was in the occupied territories. How was the Jordan Valley connected to the occupied territories? Until then, I'd had no idea. I knew that Hashomer Hatzair did not establish kibbutzim in the occupied territories, except perhaps for the one in the Golan Heights, Kibbutz Gshur, which was endlessly discussed and debated in committees and conferences, pro and con, and we all knew whether we were pro or con.

Under the heading "Everything You Wanted to Know about Gshur and Never Dared to Ask," Yoav wrote in our newsletter:

> If you object to settlements in the Golan Heights, the following is not meant for you. But if you are an open-minded person who is prepared to at least listen, the following is meant for you. In a few words, we will try to tell you Gshur's brief story.

Also, the ironic phrase "occupied territories" used by city people was a bit foreign to my ears. We called them "the territories," and it was clear that they were occupied. There was no one to argue with about that. And since there was no one to argue with about that, miraculously enough, it had vanished from my sight.

The commander said that the soldier had been outstanding during basic training, that he wanted to serve in the army, but not in the occupied territories. He said that he would be the one to try him for refusing to serve in the occupied territories, because if others tried him, he would fare much worse. In other places, in the brigade or the division, they'd impose the heaviest punishment on him. But that commander couldn't save him from additional trials. The imprisonment he would sentence him to would be only the first in a series.

What began before the sleepless night of the soldier assigned to our battalion in the Jordan Valley, who refused to serve in the occupied territories, intensified afterwards. Things seemed to happen for no reason. I didn't understand the connection between that battalion being in the Jordan Valley and the actions that were being taken, and I didn't understand why there was a debate about Gshur and no debate about other places.

One thing led to another, one thing dropped away from the other. I wanted to serve on a base close to Tel Aviv, to leave the battalion where I did nothing. To spend my nights in the city. It had nothing to do with refusal to serve. True, I said "no" to the job of clerk in battalion headquarters, and "no" to the job of clerk in company headquarters, but what is a clerk's refusal worth? It is clear, well reasoned and based on knowledge, it is in sync with the orders, it is clear and direct. I had no counter-proposal to offer, I had no just or beautiful world to go to.

I left the people I'd grown attached to in the battalion, and was alone again. I arrived at a maintenance base in Tel Hashomer, outside of Tel Aviv.

Waiting on line to be interviewed for assignment to the maintenance base, I met Benny, who had lived on a Kibbutz in Emek Yizreel as an "outside child," not the child of kibbutz members.

That's what he told me when we met. Then an idea came to us while we were waiting: to suggest to the interviewer that we be made the base gardeners; we'd give their neglected base a beautiful garden. We said it first as a joke, as a kind of metaphor for the absurdities of the army, though we couldn't really find what we were comparing it to. We agreed that each of us, when our turn came, would suggest it to the interviewer. We'd try. The interviewer agreed at once, saying that it was an excellent idea.

From that moment on, I didn't even have a daily schedule to hold on to. We came to the base whenever we wanted to, explaining that with gardening, things were seasonal, that too much meant too little and could only hurt. We said that we'd be sure to be there for every duty assignment we were given, but there should be no special times to work in the garden. They accepted that. We planted small, beautiful gardens throughout the base, on a miniscule purchasing budget. Everyone was satisfied. And most of our time was our own.

We met in the evenings—the kibbutz soldiers serving in the city—in the apartment above the slaughterhouse in Givat Shmuel that the kibbutz rented for us. We were thrilled to see each other in the evenings. As if we'd run away from the children's houses, as if for a moment, we were again Noriko-san, the girl from Japan; we didn't have to explain anything, there were no city kids there, everything was clear; we drank instant coffee with three teaspoons of sugar, sitting on broken chairs around an invisible campfire in the living room, and we went out to see movies and talked about our day in the army. The city cockroaches crawled through the cabinets and on the kitchen counter, the city cows in the slaughterhouse bellowed their weeping all night in human voices—we knew that they knew they were going to the slaughter.

We felt that something amiss was creeping under our gardens on the base, that something had been ripped out of our crazy daily routine; I decided to go to the mental health officer; I wanted to ask her whether I needed to do something else, whether, despite everything, I needed to believe that what we were doing there had meaning, and what were Benny and I doing there anyway? I felt that the joke we'd made was coming straight back at us and was about to run over us in revenge.

I appeared in front of the health officer, who wore a uniform and had a high rank, in Tel Hashomer, near my base, and stammered out my strange, patchwork history in the army. She listened and made only one remark: "Forget it, the army is not for you."

At first, I was frightened; I thought she saw a terrible prognosis, some latent madness, let's say, and didn't want to tell me or take the responsibility upon herself. But she said no, it was too bad, there had been no way of knowing, but the army didn't suit everyone.

"But the kibbutz, and my parents, what will they say," I said. "It's not so easy to explain."

She would talk to my parents and explain it to them, the mental health officer said. And she did.

A week later, I was discharged on the day the male soldiers were discharged, partly hoping to die, partly hoping to find a new life, when I appeared at the induction center and returned the trappings of a life that had never been mine anyway.

But what would happen to me now? What would they say on the kibbutz?

My discharge from the army was never explained. It was a dramatic event for those times, and for the kibbutz. No one ever asked me point blank to explain, except for once, when Yochai, my brother, drove me to a meeting I had been invited to and came inside with me. As usual with such meetings on the kibbutz, it was not completely formal. I don't remember where we drove and who was there, only that it took place on another kibbutz. It was clearly partly a conversation and partly an inquiry, someone who was trying to sniff out whether there was some kind of insanity involved, and maybe help was needed. And if not, alternately, maybe a reprimand was in order, either overt or covert.

My brother—who had been an outstanding officer in the artillery corps, and was already working on the kibbutz and had a good reputation—was the intermediary. He fielded the questions that spun around in the air. I didn't speak. I was asked many questions on the kibbutz as well, but more in a tone that was almost concerned and implied a desire to know. With no rebuke.

My discharge had no explanation. But if it did, it wasn't psychological, so I didn't ask my parents what the mental health officer who wanted to help me had told them. Clearly, the explanation wasn't geological either; after all, there had been no earthquake; it was I who had cracked.

Perhaps the explanation was zoological, as if the rib that held us together—the Narcissus children, the Seagull children, the Ramat Gan commune children, all the Hashomer Hatzair children—had broken and I was suddenly alone, without anyone who knew me all my life, from my time in the babies' house, to the right or left of me, in front or behind me.

Maybe the explanation was geometric, as if I'd gotten lost in open space after we'd always lived in the same bounded places, with the same questions.

Questions had no answers now, as if we'd shouted to the hills the way Eliezer and Rivka had taught us to do on our walks to Tree Hill, so we could hear the echo come back to us. We shouted, but the echo no longer came back from anywhere.

18

At twenty-one, the eternal age of the volunteers who came to us from all over the world for several weeks of work and then returned to their countries, we had to choose one of three possibilities, about which an endless number of rules and regulations had been made.

The first possibility: choose freely to live in the socialist experiment. Even though we were born in it, were children of the system and the place, and even though we knew nothing about any other kind of life, we were supposed to choose, of our own free will, to be in it. After all, on the kibbutz we lived by free choice, voluntarily, not by coercion, like in the totalitarian Communist regimes of the Soviet Union, China or Hungary.

The second possibility: take a year off to work in the regional kibbutz factories among the salaried workers, as the privileged children of the factory managers. The money we earned would not be sent to the kibbutz, but an exception would be made, and we could keep it to pay for a trip abroad.

The third possibility: leave.

We left.

In an instant, we were transformed from children of the kibbutz to the ones who left it.

It was that the kibbutz "children" left, not the communal sleep issue, that tore the kibbutzim apart. The parents' inability to help their children broke their spirits. The blankets that had irritated them in their beds back when they parted from their children in the hospital could no longer cover them. Their feet remained planted in their voluntary lives, but their hearts leaped out of the kibbutz, beyond the fence, to their children, or to their own youth, which had been left behind. They wandered through their present lives as bereaved parents, wanting one thing more than anything else: to help their children. The rift occurred everywhere. Only a very small number of families were not split apart. Nearly half the kibbutzim children left during that period, some to other kibbutzim, most to cities.

We didn't blame our parents for anything. On the contrary. We took the iron double beds that Feivel made for all of us in the metalwork shop when we were in the eleventh grade; we took the double bed sheets we received from the *communa*, a double blanket, two pillows, and left. With a happy heart, but an aching conscience.

A kibbutz is not a village in a pastoral setting, filled with colorful characters, chickens and Judas trees. It is a political act, and we defected. We weren't traitors, as the ones who'd left ten years earlier, when my oldest brother did, were called; we tiptoed out quietly. We moved beyond the fence, to the place where jackals roamed, and from then on, every visit to our biological parents was a return to what had been the entire setting of our lives.

People who leave home return from time to time to see their family. But with us, it was neither a return nor a visit. The gate—that's what they call the entrance to the kibbutz where the guard was posted. The gate, which had one meaning when we lived on the kibbutz, had another, totally different, almost opposite meaning, when we left.

Would the rotating guard recognize us? Should we get out of the car and say hello to him? Should we introduce the people with us? We always got stuck at the gate, as if we were sneaking in. And on every trip to Yehiam, the pounding of our frightened hearts could be heard on all the kibbutzim.

We were among the almost 50,000 people who were born and educated on the Hashomer Hatzair kibbutzim from the time the movement was founded until the end of the era of communal sleeping in the 1990s. We were among another 100,000 children who were members of other kibbutz movements. A total of 150,000 children who grew into adulthood in fifty or seventy years (depending on the particular ideological group and the movement).

Add to that the number of adults who founded the kibbutzim, most of them parents of those children, and others who joined the core groups and youth movements. Some of them left at the beginning, some left later, some were killed in war or committed suicide; most of the founders have already died.

Only these few experienced one of the most extraordinary experiments ever carried out, freely and independently chosen, to build a different world that required a different concept of family and a different concept of home.

But why would a person leave his home and continue to speak only about it? And how he left it? And how he betrayed it? Even after we left, we constantly told each other the myth of our new world creation, the experiment that did not succeed.

Those who left the kibbutz remained, in some sense, part of it. Their new identity as "the ones who left the kibbutz" kept them bound to it, and symbolized, just as their names on the clothes from the *communa* had, that they still belonged.

Since the kibbutz is an enterprise focused on "doing," and as such is by nature optimistic and productive, those who remained did not go under when others left. The moment their leaving became a fact, the ones who remained adjusted to it and considered those who left ambassadors of a sort to the urban world. That strange attitude was shared by both groups to a great extent.

Many years before we left, we heard about the others who had left far back in the past. In the Children's Society, we were proud of them without even having known them. We knew about them through stories that circulated among us and might have been rumors, gossip, or folk tales. We, the children, constantly told each other stories with inaccurate plots and distorted details as if they were necklaces of plastic beads pretending to be glass. Bits of legends blended together in our minds, and sometimes the tail ends of stories about one person were stuck onto a different person.

We were particularly proud of Arik Lavie, the popular singer.

We were careful to tell only the parts of his story that were true in order to preserve its brief, fragile existence in our world. The "in our world" is quite exaggerated, since he left once and for all in 1948, twelve years before we were born. He was here at the very beginning, when the entire kibbutz was in Kiryat Haim (and was not yet called Yehiam, but Hasela) and all the members earned their livings working outside it. Arik Lavie had a good profession and earned well—he was an engraver, and like all the members, gave his salary to the kibbutz. He took his second month's salary and left. But he came back when half the kibbutz was already in the fortress, during the war. He was there on Passover, 1948, during the siege. He taunted Qawugji's snipers, who were on Tree Hill. He would climb the wall and shout "Ya'alah Muhmad!" then jump down quickly as the sound of the snipers' bullets whistled through the air.

None of us had ever seen Shmuel Amir, who left many years before we were born and lived abroad. He apparently did well in business, but in our stories, he was a multi-millionaire who bought skyscrapers, estates, and finally entire cities in the United States, or according to another version, in Canada.

We monitored the radio, waiting to hear famous former members of Yehiam speak. Surely they would talk about the most important thing, the period when their life was shaped on Kibbutz Yehiam.

And if those who left us did not mention Yehiam, we were afraid that those might be only stories. Perhaps they never happened on Yehiam. Perhaps Arik Lavie never stole a tractor, or shot at Tree Hill, or left because they wouldn't let him study opera. After all, he didn't mention it in the interview.

But the not too distant future would arrive like a changing

season of the year, and again sweeten the stories, proving that everything was absolutely true, that we had seen only the tip of the iceberg. For example, when Arik Lavie, after becoming a famous singer, came to perform at a kibbutz anniversary celebration, thus retroactively affirming all the stories about those who had left: the singer Chava Alberstein, who was here for a week in the army; Gidon Reicher, the TV personality, who was in the Jerusalem core group; Misha Asherov, the actor, who was on the kibbutz when it was founded, and others.

We believed that since they left, they had each been acting as a city commune with a single member. There, in large cities or throughout the world, they were spreading the ideas of equality and justice, and more importantly, they were talking about the actual existence of Kibbutz Yehiam, five minutes from the end of the world. They earned their money, like their reputations, for us, for the time we would need them. At the moment of truth, they would all return to us, would contribute their formidable fortunes to the kibbutz, and come to lend a hand on the banana plantations.

The beauty of our kibbutz was incredible. We could never get used to it. We all felt unworthy of it and the system. Who could say no to an attempt to create a better, egalitarian, just world? We didn't say no. We defected.

Before we left, we went back to the kibbutz for a "conscience year." We felt that we had to give back. Though you cannot really give back, our debt was boundless, stretching from the coastline to the sky, from Yanuh to Petra. But we wanted to reduce it. A year off from the kibbutz seemed to us to be a crater of new debt; we told the French secretary that we wouldn't take it. We also said no to studying at the university for a degree, which he suggested. And no to driving lessons. We wanted to stop owing, to stop accumulating more and more debts.

During my conscience year on the kibbutz, I met Andrew. He worked on the banana plantation and in the dining hall, washing dishes, and anywhere else the emissary of our conscience, the work scheduler presently on his yearly rotation who would suddenly appear in front of us everywhere, all the time, told him to. The banana plantation was considered the most prestigious branch on the kibbutz, not only because it was productive and profitable, but also because the work was the most difficult. They told us that some of the kibbutzim in the Jordan Valley engraved a bunch of bananas on the headstones of the banana workers who passed away. On our small kibbutz of four or five hundred people, everyone knew who was a good worker.

The title "A Good Worker on the Banana Plantation" was not bestowed on those who did good work on the banana plantation, but only on those who went to work during hailstorms, those who cared about breaking harvest records, packing records, records for the size of bunches; it was bestowed on those who loaded bunches on their back all season and knew how to pile them properly on the tractor carts.

Andrew arrived unvaccinated, caught the conscience disease from us and worked in an effort to satisfy the system. Not only was he a good worker, an excellent worker, but he also seemed to carry around inside him the symbolic medal of valor that was tattooed on our heart—"Conscientious." We worked out of a guilty conscience for a system that would never be satisfied. We felt as if our conscience was a biological, organic part of our body, like an invisible inner hump.

Andrew was older than most of the volunteers, about thirty, and stayed on Yehiam longer than most of them. He left and came back, left and came back, like a lost son. He was the son of a strict captain who spent his entire life on ships, a father who drank whiskey instead of water. Andrew had been educated in Spartan boarding schools. On Kibbutz Yehiam, he felt at home for the first time in his life.

My departure for Tel Aviv had already been arranged, but I postponed it for a year in order to work on the kibbutz, like a pathetic penitent for something for which there was no repentance: my approaching desertion. Andrew also knew that he had to return to Scotland, forever.

Yael in Tel Aviv, 1980.

At the end of that year, I went abroad for the first time. Neither as a city person nor as a kibbutznik. I went as part of my job as a double agent, as an escort to Avital, a girl in a group I worked with during that conscience year. Her father, who had been in the French core group, left the kibbutz and went back to Paris. He was anxious for her to visit him there during the summer vacation, that is, the *vacances*. She was afraid of going abroad, of Paris, of the family, of the *vacances*. On the kibbutz, there was no family and no *vacances*. We worked full time for two thirds of the summer vacation, and went to the movement camp on the Sea of Galilee or the Jordan River for the remaining time. She wanted someone to look out for her, and took me. She was no less a part of my leaving the kibbutz than I was part of her visit to her father, who had left a long time ago. On the plane, she said that she could actually manage by herself and just wanted me to stay close to her. There, in Paris, her father arranged an apartment for me to live in. I woke up every morning to a world spun from imagination: tiled sidewalks, streetlamps, beauty that was immersed in soft gray light, so different from our constantly blazing sun. I woke up every morning to buy a croissant. And during that month, while Avital was still spending time with her father, I went to visit Andrew, who had returned to Glasgow, this time forever. He sent me a ticket for a luxurious bus that went from London to Glasgow, to come and visit him. I took the bus, but felt like Ayelet, who flew on the wings of her imagination in our favorite Kadya Molodovski poem:

Far away in Warsaw,
A marsh, a yard, a house.

There lives Ayelet, pretty girl,
With her blue parasol.

[...]

Ayelet longs to wander with the larks,
Until the day grows very, very dark.

Her mother calls out to the girl,
The windows chime and ring.

The father, black from soot,
Bangs his hammer as he calls:
Hurry home!
There is thread to be woven,
Patches to be darned,
Knots to be tied,
And buttons to be sewn.

[...]

Ayelet hitches wheels in a row,
And makes a train that travels to and fro.

The whistle blows, Ayelet goes,
Off to which distant lands – who knows?

I turned my head on the luxurious London-Glasgow bus to Glasgow to see who was calling me, who knew that I was there. And for a moment, I realized that no one was calling me to go back to work, no one was calling me at all. For the first time in my life, I was free.

I stayed in the huge, gorgeous, remodeled apartment where Andrew, his brother and a friend lived—the three of them were artists and architects who had designed it. They gave me my own room, a room with gilded walls and a huge bed, white sheets and fluffy pillows. The ceiling was very high and strewn with stars that they had molded into it. I lived in an apartment with three men, in my own room, on my own floor. Everything was different. They climbed a ladder into a pantry to take down enough sugar for the three teaspoonfuls I took. They never used sugar and loathed instant coffee, the sweet drug of our lives. We went to pubs and plays and to see the houses planned and built by Mackintosh, the Scottish architect. We went to Edinburgh to see a play, and they took me to see their parents in their kilts, and to visit their architect friends. I moved awkwardly in nice-to-meet-you hugs. We didn't hug and kiss on the kibbutz. During the city hugs and kisses, we stopped breathing, executed our roles in the coerced, artificial choreography for what seemed an eternity. We didn't hug our parents, our biological siblings or our fellow group members. Only the urbanites, and only if we had to.

We talked until morning. They ordered Indian food and asked me: hot or medium? I said hot. They asked again, politely, if I was sure. I said yes, of course, and thought, they're weird, these Scots. Hot, let it cool off. But it was spicy, and they laughed endlessly about the mistakes I could never anticipate. I had no idea about food or about English. After all, we didn't have to learn. We didn't know anything. Not Arabic, not English, not Hebrew.

On the way back, waiting in line for the ferry in Dover, someone struck up a conversation with me, asking in stilted English, "Haven't I didn't meeting you in Ireland?" I recognized him; he was a year or two older than I was, but one of the people who had built the movement's acclaimed zip lines. After completing his official job, he'd volunteered to build long, twisting zip lines for others, which would begin at the skyscraping tops of eucalyptus trees, and end at the Jordan River.

I replied in Hebrew: "We must have met at a zip line; a beam must have fallen on us and that's where we know each other from, not from Ireland." He recognized me, and I remembered his name. Shmuel. He looked like a man who had descended the Eiffel Tower on a zip line. Shorts, high shoes, a wallet sticking out of his back pocket, a wallet that would be stolen from him on his first metro ride in the city. He was going to Paris, he said, he didn't know anyone. He had no place to live.

Our city apartment was never ours. It was at the disposal of the entire movement. And even if Dov, Avital's father, left Yehiam a long time ago and returned to Paris after giving up on the possibility of building a new, progressive world, he certainly had to know that he couldn't say no.

I have a place, I told Shmuel, filled with guilt about the luxurious circumstances of my life, made possible by the kibbutz and by Dov, Avital's father. I told him that he could sleep in my apartment on the fifth floor, the attic apartment that Dov gave me for a month, but not in bed with me. But actually, there was no other bed there, and not even a kitchen. Okay, so with me, but no touching. That was acceptable among us, among our fellow group members. Although he did not grow up with us in Narcissus or Seagull, he was exactly like us.

Thanks to Avri Sela

The newsletter and archives on Yehiam were Avri, and Avri was the newsletter and archives. Their histories are intertwined. Avri began writing and editing the newsletter when the kibbutz was still in Kiryat Haim, in 1946, before Yehiam was settled. From then until he passed away on Yehiam, Avri edited the newsletter and collected every note posted on the bulletin board and every piece of paper that anyone read from, even before they finished reading it. Many members preferred to make a copy of everything they wrote in advance, fearing that Avri would take down their notices too soon.

To help me write this book, Avri placed at my disposal everything he had collected, organized and cherished for decades—the newsletters and the entire contents of the archives. He was always happy to do it, inspired by curiosity and his love for what he did. Avri died a few months before I finished writing the book. I thank him with all my heart.

REFERENCES

The poem "We picked meadow flowers today" on page 38 is taken from the book, *Poems—With a Blue Flower in My Lapel* by Oded Burla, published by Danny Books, 2008.

The quotations on pages 40, 46 and 50 are taken from the book *1967—Israel, the War, and the Year that Transformed the Middle East* by Tom Segev, published by Keter Publishing, 2005.

The quotation on page 76 is taken from the book *From the Edge of the East and Deep in the Heart* by Mordechai Shachevitz, published by Gderot Publishers 1992.

The poem on page 107 is taken from the book *What Do the Does Do—Poems for Children* by Leah Goldberg, published by Sifriat Poalim, 1957.

The poem "Parting," on page 200 by Gabriel Priel, is taken from an article by Menachem Perry printed in *Siman Kria* 9, 1979.

The poem, "Evening Opposite Gilad," quoted on page 217 is taken from the book *What Do the Does Do—Poems for Children* by Leah Goldberg, published by Sefriat Poalim, 1957.

The poem on page 240 is taken from the book *They Opened the Door* by Kadya Molodowsky, published by Kibbutz Hameuchad Publishers, 1946.